On Stony Ground

Brenda Lee-Whiting

Juniper Books

Published by Juniper Books,
R.R.2, Renfrew, Ont. K7V 3Z5, Canada

ISBN 0-919137-15-6

Printed and bound in Canada.

Copyright (c) 1986, Brenda B. Lee-Whiting.
No part of this book may be reproduced or transmitted by any means, including photocopying, without written permission from the publisher, with the exception of brief passages quoted for review purposes.

Photographs.
All photographs in this book, with the exception of those otherwise credited, were taken by Brenda Lee-Whiting. These photos may not be copied ,or used for any other purpose, without the written consent of the author.

Canadian Cataloguing in Publication Data

Lee-Whiting, Brenda, 1929-
  On stony ground

Includes index.
ISBN 0-919137-15-6

1. Germans--Ontario--Renfrew (County)--History.
2. German Canadians--Ontario--Renfrew (County)--History. 3. Frontier and pioneer life--Ontario--Renfrew (County) 4. Germans--Ontario--Renfrew (County)--History--Pictorial works. 5. German Canadians--Ontario--Renfrew (County)--History--Pictorial works. 6. Frontier and pioneer life--Ontario--Renfrew (County)--Pictorial works.
I. Title.

FC3095.R4Z7 1986   971.3'8100431   C86-090169-6
F1059.R4L44 1986

Cover photo

GRAIN CRADLE
The third owner of a Century Farm, Matthew Noack III of Hagarty Township, fetches the grain cradle out of the granary. An extension with long wooden fingers was added to a scythe to convert it into a cradle. Swung by a reaper, the cradle cut a swath of grain and laid it neatly in rows where it could be bound into sheaves by a farmer's wife or the children. On small farms the labour of a large family was more economical than the mechanized reaping machines that were introduced in the latter half of the 19th century. This cradle was used by Mr. Noack as late as the 1920s in fields where boulders would have made it difficult to use machines.

Contents

Chapter I.
Newcomers from Germany   7

Chapter II.
Settling into a new country   19

Chapter III.
Keeping warm and fed   39

Chapter IV.
Furnishing the home   64

Chapter V.
Signs of change   85

Selected obituaries   111

Index.   116

Preface

My interest in photographing items that had been made by the German immigrants who came to Renfrew County in the years following 1858, led me into many homes, rural and urban, during the period since 1977 when I began to make intensive records. Being allowed to borrow old documents and old photographs, so that reproductions could be made, involved trust; being permitted to photograph personal objects that were still in use and still treasured, involved discretion. I was well aware that I was a guest who had to observe certain proprieties. If there are some photographs in this book that describe the object as being in a certain township, without further identification, then the reader must realise that to make known the name and address of the owner would break a confidence.

Discretion can be provided and accuracy maintained in some cases by naming the original owner and original location. For example, the dish cupboard made for Julius Haas in Locksley, most probably by Johann Noack (1839-1919), was photographed at the home of the granddaughter who lives in Pembroke and whose married surname is not Haas.

Very often my visit to a home was prompted by the advertisement of an auction sale which was to be held soon, and I tried to call at the home several days before the event. I knew that the family would be too busy on the day of the auction to answer questions, and it was easier to take photographs when there was no crowd of bidders blocking the view. If the item was to be sold to the highest bidder, then it has changed hands many times since I photographed it and there should be no harrassment possible if its original location is given. Making a visit to a home that was about to be cleared out by an auction often had fringe benefits too, for there might be items that the family members were withholding from sale and dispersing among themselves. Some of these items were captured on film before they made their journey out of the county to distant places in Canada and the United States. There had to be a guarantee of privacy if the owners wished it, and said so, and this was especially needed if the owners were collectors who had purchased the item from an antique dealer or from a member of a German family, without perhaps consulting other members.

Some readers may feel that certain German families have been mentioned more than once, in the text and/or photographs, while others have been left out. This is certainly true. Those who got in touch with me, after I had advertised my interest in several weekly newspapers in Renfrew County, were the most likely to be visited. Finding homes that held objects of the past was a matter of chance and luck, with one householder often telling me about another person of his acquaintance who possessed something that I was looking for.

There has been some confusion regarding the year in which the German-speaking immigrants first arrived in Renfrew County. Written records in the archives show 1858 as the first year that German farmers actually settled and cleared land in this "settlement on the Ottawa". On the other hand, some families are certain that their ancestors came in 1857, the first year that the Canadian government advertised in Germany that newcomers to the vicinity of the colonization roads in eastern Ontario could obtain land without fee or for small sums of money.

One descendant, who purposefully pursued his "roots" in Germany and Poland in the fall of 1985, has gained solid answers to the question for his family at least. Russel E. Witt, a great-grandson of Friedrich Witt, visited the Historic Emigration Office in The Museum of Hamburg History, at Hostenwall 24, 2000 Hamburg 36, with an enquiry about ships that sailed from that port in the spring of 1857. Within an hour, and for a fee of $35 U.S., Mr. Witt received a photo-copy of the page from the Passenger List, which contained details of his ancestor's family. This included names, ages, occupations and the birthplaces of all members, plus the name of the ship (Copernicus), the destination (Quebec) and the date of the ship's sailing, April 1, 1857. On the same page of this Copernicus Passenger List appear the names of Christian Beisenthal and some other names familiar in Renfrew County, such as Mau and Schultz.

The sailing date of April 1 is significant as it fits the suggestion from Crown Lands Agent, T.P. French, that immigrants should arrive in the early part of the summer, in order to have full advantage of the growing season. It is exactly the same date as that recorded on the 1863 ship's contract signed by the Horcun (Okum) family, when they sailed from the same port of Hamburg six years later to Canada. Information revealed in that contract is included in this book, which is designed to add to the published knowledge of the German settlement in Renfrew county.

Brenda B. Lee-Whiting,
P.O. Box 467,
DEEP RIVER, Ontario
K0J 1P0

GERMAN CONFEDERATION, 1815–1866

NOTE. Numbered states are as follows: (1) Lauenburg; (2) Mecklenburg-Strelitz; (3) Mecklenburg-Schwerin; (4) Schaumburg-Lippe; (5) Lippe; (6) Brunswick; (7) Anhalt; (8) Schwarzburg-Sondershausen; (9) Waldeck; (10) Saxe-Coburg-Gotha; (11) Saxe-Weimar; (12) Saxe-Meiningen; (13) Reuss, Elder and Younger; (14) Saxe-Altenburg; (15) Hohenzollern-Sigmaringen; (16) Liechtenstein. In Luxemburg and Limburg, the dotted line shows the boundary of the Confederation after 1839.

Chapter I.

Newcomers from Germany

On Walling's Map of 1863, there is no sign of the communities in Renfrew County where German-speaking immigrants would leave their mark. There are places with British names like Pembroke, Renfrew and Douglas; there are villages named after British pioneers such as Eganville and Forester's Falls. There is even one community with an Indian name, Osceola, and there are some that commemorate geographical features, such as Lake Dore and Mt. St. Patrick.

Although German immigrants began to settle on land in the rural townships of this county in 1858, many years would elapse before the post offices that served these newcomers who spoke in a foreign tongue would reflect the presence of the German people. When the 1861 census was conducted in Renfrew County, the numbers of German-speaking residents were not large enough to warrant a separate entry in the records. The federal census-takers of that year combined the totals of those who declared Germany, Holland or Prussia as their native land or ethnic origin. For Renfrew County the tally was 405, and it must have included the 56 households of German-speaking immigrants that had been listed by a government immigration agent, William Sinn, in the fall of 1860, when he was sent to the Ottawa Valley to report on the progress of the "Prussian settlement".

Both federal census-takers and immigration agents were understandably confused by some German-speaking residents who gave Germany as their native land and others who claimed that they had come from Prussia. There were others who declared themselves as Prussians, although they were Polish-speaking.

When the Canadian government began to advertise on the continent of Europe in 1857, hoping to attract immigrants to fill up the unsettled areas of Upper Canada, Germany consisted of a loose association of 28 autonomous states called the German Confederation. The largest state was the Kingdom of Prussia, (see map), which was divided into eight provinces, one of which was called the province of Prussia (formed when the provinces of West Prussia and East Prussia were united). Of the remaining seven provinces, the other one that was losing much of its population to immigration at that time was Pomerania — which is today divided between East Germany and Poland. Other Prussian provinces which were visited by William Wagner, 1860-62, an immigration agent from Canada, and which contributed significant numbers of people to Renfrew County, were Brandenburg, Silesia and Posen. In 1866, another immigration agent, a Mr. Bechel, who was sent by a private land speculation company, travelled through other German provinces, such as Hanover and Hesse-Cassel, and reported to his employers that he had convinced some residents there to choose Canada as their destination overseas.

Following the unification of Germany in 1870, immigration continued from that country, fuelled by the fear that three wars in seven years had enflamed. Though Germany remained peaceful in succeeding decades, those who left this country to make a new life in Canada continued to regard themselves as natives of provinces or states which no longer had a separate existence. When Charlotte Auguste Zadow Zillmer died April 21, 1905, and was buried in Eganville, her tombstone described her as a native of Pommern (the German word for Pomerania), although this widowed immigrant left Germany with her family in 1881.

In the federal census that was taken in 1881, the number of residents that claimed German as their ethnic origin was 4,831 in Renfrew County, but much of this figure was due to natural increase. The census of 1871 showed that the numbers of German people in this county had risen to 2,318, most of them young adults with young children, who had braved the Atlantic crossing in a decade when sailing ships from Germany took many weeks to complete the passage. Descendants of the first wave of immigrants from Germany believe that anywhere from seven to thirteen weeks was common. The time of arrival was unpredictable.

Sailing ships bound for Canada left Germany early in the season, for the immigration agents had stressed that the settlers should arrive in time to tackle the jobs of clearing the land and planting crops.

When Matthew Horcun with his wife and three children, set sail from Hamburg, Germany, April 1, 1863, bound for the port of Quebec in Canada, he did not know the full extent of the difficulties that he would face in the New World. He did know what to expect during the ocean voyage on the ship, *Gellert*, because the 'ship's contract' (Schiffs-Contract) which he had signed jointly with C. Eisenstein of Berlin, an agent from Donati & Co. of Hamburg, March 28, spelled out the conditions, services and provisions in great detail. Two copies of this contract were made, to be retained by both parties. The original copy held by the Horcun family is still in the possession of the great-grandson, Keith Schleuter, who continues to live and work on the land in Hagarty Township, Renfrew County, where his ancestor settled.

The Royal Prussian Ministry for trade, business, etc. and the Government of the City of Hamburg gave their approval and the dignity of their names to the contracts drawn up for Robert M. Sloman's ships. These vessels, which were subject to local regulations, had been appointed for the acceptance and the transportation of emigrants, non-stop, to destinations that included New York, Quebec, New Orleans, Galveston, Port Adelaide, Sydney and Melbourne.

The Horcuns sailed on a vessel under the command of an experienced seaman, Captain Terry, who had made the transatlantic voyage several times before. The 32-year-old emigrant, with his wife, Anna, 35, and daughters, Lise, 9, Anna, 6, and Maria, 4, travelled in the lower deck or steerage; for each adult, 28 thaler was the price of the crossing, and for children under ten years the payment was 22 thaler. For infant nurslings, who were less than 12 months old at the commencement of the voyage, the cost was three thaler. The age of the children had to be proved by passports, which the passengers had to obtain before boarding. Only a deposit was needed when the contract was signed, but the rest of the passage money had to be paid two days before the scheduled date of departure, along with 72 RC in Prussian funds.

Emigrants had to pay their own way to Hamburg. Before the ship sailed, they had to equip themselves with their own mattresses or beds, blankets, vessels for eating, drinking and washing, as well as their own knives, forks and spoons. They were also responsible for marking their baggage with their names, loading it on to the ship, and taking care of it during the voyage. There was no compensation for lost effects.

Those who signed the contract agreed to stay at appointed lodgings in Hamburg. After seeing their families safely installed, the fathers of families had to report, without delay, to a bursar at a given address. Once aboard the ship, passengers had given their promise that the orders of the captain or helmsman would be obeyed, and they also contracted to obey the laws in the ports where they disembarked.

Complete food for the entire trip, from the day of boarding to the day of landing at destination, was included in the passage price. According to local regulations, this consisted of: ½ lb. meat daily, either beef or pork; once a week this may be replaced by a daily ration of two herrings; ½ lb. of peas, beans, barley, lentils, baked goods (from flour), sauerkraut or similar food; morning coffee; evening tea; 5 lbs. bread and $5/12$ lb. butter weekly; a sufficient quantity of good pure drinking water, potatoes, plums, vinegar, and so forth will likewise be supplied by us and the men will be dispensed a shot of brandy every morning. The sick receive food beneficial to them (wine, sago, gruel, etc.) as well as any necessary medication from the Ship's Apothecary. All foods will be distributed, cooked and prepared. Each person over 10 years receives a full portion, children from one to 10 receive half portion."

After arrival of the ship at its destination, room and board was provided for two days. The contract included any fee charged in America for entry or admission to hospital. For each passenger paying full fare the accompanying luggage allowance was 20 cubic feet, and 10 cubic feet for a child. For each additional cubic foot the charge to the American ports was 1½ Rf, and the charge to Australian ports was 1 Rf, to be paid in Hamburg before departure.

In 1863, the year that the Horcuns travelled on the *Gellert*, the proportion of immigrants who crossed the Atlantic Ocean on sailing ships was 54%. In fact, the shipping service between Hamburg and Quebec ended in 1871, although sea travel continued from Germany to New York after that date. More and more, the immigrants who journeyed from Germany to Canada were crossing the ocean in steamships; they had the advantage of faster travel, which in turn, reduced the risks of diseases that spread through crowded ships. Gustav and Caroline Michel, who left Silesia in 1867, were bereaved by the death of all three children during their lengthy sailing voyage that year, but after their settlement in Petawawa Township had three sons. By 1869 the number of immigrants who travelled to Canada by steamship had risen to 95%, and in 1875 all newcomers journeyed in ships powered by coal-fired boilers, instead of the uncertain wind.

A surprising number of the descendants of German immigrants who came to Renfrew County in the second half of the 19th century know the name of the ship that brought their ancestors to Canada. Few are aware that those who made the journey in the last 30 years of that century (and some before 1870) boarded a British steamship at Liverpool, England. The company that dominated the shipping lanes between Britain and North America during the last three decades of the 19th century and well into the 20th was the Montreal Ocean Steamship Company, later known as the Allan Line, which was incorporated by an Act of the Canadian Parliament, Dec. 18, 1854. The company had its principal office in the Alexandra Buildings, James Street, Liverpool, the English sea-port which was second only to London as "the greatest emporium of the British Empire,

FROM GERMANY TO CANADA
VIA ENGLAND IN 1874

In the Canadian Illustrated News of April 4, 1874, a series of sketches showed scenes of German emigration. This sketch is titled "Emigrants disembarking at Hull, en route for Liverpool". Hull is a port on the east coast of England, to which passengers from Germany were ferried by small steamships; they obviously had their luggage searched by customs officials before leaving the boat and only personal effects were allowed without duty. German emigrants crossed England by train and embarked on steamships of the Allan Line at Liverpool, for the journey to North America.

Public Archives Canada C-61173

THE ALLAN LINE

Sometimes known as The Montreal Ocean Steamship Company, The Allan Line was the trans-Atlantic shipping company that operated between Liverpool, England, and North American ports during the last quarter of the 19th century, bringing thousands of immigrants to Canada. The CIRCASSIAN, pictured below, was built in 1873 and travelled the Atlantic until 1896.

Built at a time when shipping companies were converting from sail to steam, the CIRCASSIAN was equipped with masts and a funnel, allowing it to take advantage of both wind and fuel.

Public Archives Canada. C-35120

GERMAN IMMIGRANT'S CHEST

This wooden chest, braced with metal straps and reinforced at the corners, contained the belongings of Julius Albert Zadow, who left Germany May 3, 1881 with his mother, wife, children, and brothers. Zadow was a trained furniture-maker who brought with him tools of his trade, such as planes and a scorp. The chest is owned by the fourth child of Albert's second marriage, but though the key is in the lock, the tools have been dispersed and shared.

and, in fact, of the world", according to McCulloch's Universal Gazeteer, an encyclopedia published in New York in 1852. Liverpool is located on the long estuary of the Mersey River and because the surrounding land is low, docks had to be constructed to protect the ships from gale winds and to facilitate the loading and unloading of merchandise. Vessels from Canada came loaded with timber, while those from the coast of Virginia and other American states brought tobacco, and cotton for the Lancashire mills. By 1852, it was estimated that Liverpool's docks covered 110 acres and the port had a quay-space that was seven and one quarter miles in length.

Hamburg, the greatest commercial city of Germany, is located on the Elbe River, but had no docks or quays at that time. Vessels drawing 14 feet of water could navigate close to the city, but had to moor in the river a short distance from shore. The shipping belonging to Hamburg was small as compared to its trade.

By 1857, the first year that the Canadian advertisements appeared in Germany, the Allan Line had eight steamships on the North Atlantic run; their names were: *Canadian, Indian, North American, Anglo-Saxon, Nova Scotian, North Briton, Hungarian* and *Bohemian*. Departures from Liverpool to Quebec and Montreal were made every second Wednesday, and the westbound passage to Quebec was made in an average time of 12 days and 14 hours. It was still primarily an era of sailing ships, as many drawings of the period, sketched on both sides of the ocean, confirm. Many German immigrants still made that crossing in a sailing ship, such as the *Copernicus*, which left Hamburg on April 1, 1857, carrying on its passenger list the names of the family of Friedrich Witt and others such as the Maus and the Biesenthals, who would first try the Kitchener County area and then pioneer in Renfrew County where land was cheaper. The transition from sail to steam was slow in the German shipping companies and the Allan Line profited as a result.

By 1870, there were small steamships of the Allan Line travelling on the Baltic Sea, in order to collect immigrants from continental Europe who were bound for the New World. From Scandinavian countries and from Germany passengers boarded these ships which took them to the east coast of England, to land at Hull, and then cross the country by train to Liverpool where they embarked on a transatlantic steamship. Referring to the Allan Line, the Canadian News of May 23, 1872, commented: "The mail steamers have run during the year with exemplary regularity and expedition, the average length of voyage westward being 11 days, 17 hours". This time included a port of call in Ireland. The passengers who arrived at Quebec were transferred with their baggage, at no extra charge, to the railway trains which came alongside the vessel at the wharf. A similar procedure was followed at Halifax, and at both ports there was an agent from the Allan Line to superintend the transfer as quickly as possible and protect passengers from the intrigues of those who would prey upon the ignorance of the newly-arrived immigrant.

All such advantages were outlined in the pamphlet that was printed by the company in 1872 titled "Practical Hints and Directions to Intending Emigrants to Canada and the United States". That year the company had the following steamships in service: *Sarmatian, Scandinavian, Prussian, Peruvian, Nestorian, Hibernian, Austrian, Germany, Moravian, Norway, Polynesian, Circassian, North American, Corinthian, Caspian, Manitobian, St. David, St. Andrew, St. Patrick* and *Sweden*. A few, like the last-named, were feeders to the Atlantic route, operating on the Baltic Sea, while others, like the *Circassian*, steamed across the Atlantic Ocean for almost a quarter of a century.

The flow of passengers from Germany that took this route was so well established by 1874 that the Canadian Illustrated News of April 4 that year published a couple of illustrations headed "German Emigration" that showed two stages of the journey. One sketch was a scene of emigrants disembarking at Hull, en route for Liverpool, while the other showed a crowded quay at Liverpool, where emigrants were boarding ships for Quebec.

In both the intermediate and steerage classes, stewardesses were appointed to attend to the comforts of female passengers and children during the voyage. The intermediate fare was £3-3-0 higher than that of the steerage fare and the menus were different, but steerage passengers were assured that they would be supplied with as much food as they could eat, all of the best quality, having been inspected beforehand by Her Majesty's Emigration Officers. Breakfast was served at 8 a.m. and consisted of coffee, sugar and fresh bread, or biscuit and butter or oatmeal porridge and molasses. The midday meal at one p.m. would contain beef or pork and soup, with bread and potatoes, or fish and potatoes, according to the day of the week, with the special treat of a pudding on Sundays. A light supper was provided at 6 p.m. with tea, sugar, biscuit and butter. Cabin fares did not include wines and liquors, but they could be obtained on board for an additional payment. There was no brandy in the morning for the men, as on the sailing ship, *Gellert*, and the provisions lacked variety, but the speed of the passage must have compensated for the dreary menus. Another advantage of the Allan Line was the presence of an experienced surgeon on all steamships that crossed the Atlantic.

By 1872 the Canada Central railway had been constructed as far as Renfrew. Some German immigrants, such as Mr. and Mrs. Wilhelm Budd who came that year, were able to take the train as far as that village on the Ottawa and Opeongo Colonization Road, and walk the remaining distance to Wilberforce Township where they settled. In later years their son, Julius, built a succession of sawmills on a creek in that township and the small community that grew around the millsite became known as Budd Mills.

By the time of the 1871 federal census the presence of the German settlers in some rural townships was second in numbers only to the Irish, but very few had settled in the villages. The census-takers listed them as follows: Arnprior village, 76; Admaston Twp., 62; Algonas (both

North and South), 179; Alice and Fraser Twps., 585; Bagot and Blythfield Twps., 25; Brougham Twp., 0; Bromley Twp., 40; Brudenell, Raglan, Radcliffe and Lyndoch Twps., 82; Grattan Twp., 56; Head Twp., 8; Horton Twp., 23; McNab Twp., 88; Matawatchan and Griffith Twps., 109; Pembroke Twp., 10; Pembroke village, 25; Petawawa Twp., 117; Renfrew village, 7; Rolph, Buchanan, Wylie and McKay Twps., 28; Ross Twp., 12; Sebastopol Twp., 201; Stafford Twp., 32; Westmeath Twp., 37; Wilberforce Twp., 625.

The German immigrants who were living in Arnprior village were laborers and their families, and one stonemason. The men who lived in the townships were nearly all described as farmers, apart from the occasional shoemaker, blacksmith or carpenter; some of the women were described as weavers. There were no school teachers or ministers among the German-speaking immigrants that settled in Renfrew County, but their need for religious guidance had attracted missionaries to the Ottawa Valley in the 1860s who could speak the German language. One diligent worker in the field, Rev. Ludwig Herman Gerndt, reported on the state of his missionary efforts, 1861-1870, to the governing body of the Lutheran Church. Though he was the resident pastor of the Wilmot German Mission (Mannheim, Dundee, Roseville and Elmira) in southern Ontario in 1861, he found time to make "several exploring tours into distant settlements of Lutherans in Canada West" and by 1865, was travelling through a region in eastern Ontario that in his estimation stretched for 150 miles in length and which was 60 miles wide.

Mr. Gerndt reported to the Synod that one of the German immigrants in the Renfrew County settlement had written to him with the following plea: "When on Sunday I sit at my window and look out over the waste field of snow and the grave of my son, I ofttimes imagine I hear the church bells of home, with their friendly tones, calling the congregation together. But, alas! Eight years have passed since we (twenty German families) have been here, without hearing a single sermon! None of our children have been confirmed! We have no consecrated God's Acre (burial place for the dead)! Each one buries his dead where it seems best, and bewails his sad loss without one comforting word from a minister of the gospel! How painfully one misses the presence of a pious pastor in circumstances of heavy sorrow . . . If we could only occasionally hear a German preacher of our faith, we would be satisfied."

Because the immigration from Germany was not prompted by religious persecution or dissent, the new arrivals were not members of a single homogenous denomination. They belonged to a variety of faiths and because most of them located in townships that were thinly populated and had no churches, the settlers from Germany organized their own congregations, within which they could worship in a familiar tongue. Those few early immigrants from Germany who chose to live in or near communities, well settled already, would find themselves in such a minority that they might gravitate

MISSIONARY'S BUGGY
When Rev. L.H. Gerndt was in charge of Lutheran congregations in Eastern Ontario, 1861-1870, he used this buggy in his travels over an extensive terrain. In Canada's Centennial Year, 1967, the congregation of St. John's Lutheran Church, Petawawa village, marked its 100th anniversary, May 14, by displaying Mr. Gerndt's buggy, which had been stored for at least 50 years on the farm of a member, Alfred Gutzman. The first Lutheran services in Petawawa in 1867 were held in the home of Gustave Michel by the missionary, who lived at Locksley, Alice Township.

to churches that were established. For example, Mr. and Mrs. William J. Michaelis, a tailor and his wife, who were the first German immigrants to settle in the village of Eganville in 1876, became members of the Presbyterian church, since there were no church services in the German language at that time in that community.

A chronicle of an earlier German settlement in Upper Canada has referred to the initiative and effectiveness of the Methodist Circuit Riders, and their success in meeting the requirements of scattered pioneers in the backwoods. Eastern Ontario was to provide them with another challenge and several congregations of Methodist churches were founded in the infant German communities and encouraged by the efforts of missionaries such as the Rev. Karl Schmidt who would travel through rough countryside. After this 'saddleback preacher' had made his reconnaisance in 1861, the Pembroke District of the Wesleyan Methodist Church sent for an ordained German-speaking minister for a more permanent appointment. Reverend Carl (or Charles) Allum, only 23 years old, was "received on trial for the German work for which he appears to have a peculiar

EARLY LUTHERAN IMMIGRANTS FROM GERMANY
By the time these pioneers were sketched in the 1890s, most of the men had beards and most of the women wore their hair drawn back from a centre parting — no matter from what country they had come.
William Frederick Wolfgram arrived in Canada, June 8, 1861, according to the records in possession of his granddaughter, so he probably came by sailing ship. By the time of the 1881 census, William and Caroline Wolfgram had five children the oldest being 16. They made their home in Germanicus, Wilberforce Township.

Ferdinand Biesenthal was only a child when he emigrated with his parents, in May 1856, from Mariendorf, Kreis Arnswalde, in the north of Germany. The family first settled at Mitchell, Ontario, and moved to Renfrew County in 1860. Ferdinand married Caroline Kulke, Oct. 9, 1873, and they had 14 children at their home in Locksley, Alice Township.

adaptation". In 1866 his appointment was confirmed for the German Mission of the Ottawa District, which stretched from Alice to Denbigh and beyond. In that year the minutes of the Pembroke District Council commented: "... this meeting is more deeply impressed than ever with the importance of supplying the German work with an ordained minister, especially as another church has forestalled us in this respect". The rival preacher, here referred to, may have been Mr. Gerndt, appointed by the Evangelical Lutheran Synod of Canada, or it may have been Rev. Peter Alles who was sent to Renfrew County by the Evangelical Association in 1865. Both these two missionaries were sponsored by German communities in southern Ontario, which had settled earlier and prospered. There was competition for souls to be saved.

Until 1883, the Methodist Church tried to supply German-speaking ministers to eastern Ontario, concentrating their labours in the townships of Alice, Wilberforce and the Algona. The small bands of followers of this church were so isolated that they tended to succumb to another German-speaking congregation that was proving more successful. In the township of Petawawa the German Methodists met in the home of Ferdinand Lindeman in 1866. They were outnumbered in this township by members of the St. John's Evangelical Lutheran Church, who formally organized a congregation in 1867. Mr. Lindeman was accepted as a member of this Lutheran congregation on May 6, 1876, and there is evidence that other members of the Methodist faith here followed suit. There were no reports that a Methodist church building was ever contemplated in this township, but in other townships the German Methodist congregations were along the first to erect a structure. Sadly, none survive.

In April 1869 the Green Lake congregation of the Wesleyan Methodist Church of Canada authorized its church trustees to purchase one acre of land from Evan Edwards for the sum of $1,000, a remarkable sum of money for those days. The trustees were August Lang, Jacob Boshard, Herman Yant, Charles Frederick, Martin Boudrick, August Neuman, Christopher Zebel and Wilhelm Fitzner, all of Wilberforce Township, and John Gries of Bromley Township. The log church built on this site has disappeared. By this time Mr. Allum had been joined in his endeavours by a second German-speaking Methodist minister, Rev. Stephen Kappele and it was he who witnessed the deed for the purchase of the church site.

Despite such a promising start, the efforts to establish Methodist churches among the German-speaking communities were abandoned soon after 1875. In that year, the Pembroke District Council meeting minutes record that the difficulties of obtaining ministers who could speak the language of the German immigrants caused the church to withdraw in favour of the Evangelical Association. The Methodists in Arnprior sold their church to the Evangelicals in 1882. Services were discontinued in Combermere in the 1890s, although the church was used as a place of worship until 1928. Other churches were burned or moved or demolished and not replaced.

Whether any of the German immigrants were Methodists before they left Germany, or whether they became Methodists after they settled in Renfrew County, is a question that has been debated by scholars. Certainly some of the newcomers who located in the Eganville area decided to join the Anglican church, because they found themselves without clergy to direct their spiritual life. Families such as the Buckwalds and the Bimms joined St. John the Evangelist in Eganville, while the Giermans and the family of August H.J. Schultz joined St. Clement's, the first Anglican church on the Ottawa and Opeongo Road, in nearby Grattan Township. Before the construction of the building of St. Clement's in 1892, the congregation used to be visited by a bishop who held Sunday morning services in the residence of Gottliep Gierman and his two sons from Prenzlau, Germany.

Though the influx of German-speaking immigrants into Renfrew County represented many Protestant denominations, including Baptists, and a minority of Roman Catholic families, the general impression of observers at that time and even today is that the newcomers were mainly Lutherans. Very little news about the immigrants from Germany was published in the weekly newspapers of the Ottawa Valley at that time, probably because of the language barrier, but the following item, printed in small type on the front page of The Pembroke Observer, Sept. 14, 1888, is fairly typical.

"GATHERING OF GERMANS"

"There was a great mission gathering of Germans belonging to the Lutheran Church at the church in South Alice, about seven miles from Pembroke, on Sunday last, the services lasting all day. People were there from Pembroke, Pettewawa (sic), Wilberforce, Eganville, Golden Lake and other distant places, and with the congregation of the neighbourhood made up an assemblage of many hundreds. The mission appears to be an annual one, and lasts but one day. Last year we believe it was held somewhere above Eganville. No doubt this year it was more successful than on any previous occasion. Of course the church would have been much too small to give those assembled even standing room, and the services were accordingly held in the woods close by. Everything had been thoroughly prepared for a good field meeting and a good one there was. Three clergymen were present, one of them being from Ottawa, the other two from this section. Two good choirs were present, one from Wilberforce and one from Alice. In addition to leading the assemblage in singing, each of the choirs gave choruses at different times. There were services in the forenoon and services in the afternoon. The prayers were solemn and hearty, the sermons were long and devout, and the singing was really good.

All the services were of course entirely in German. The people of the neighbourhood generally entertained those from a distance. The assemblage was a most interesting one, being composed of Germans of all descriptions from the Pembroke lady in her silk dress and all the modern style to the recent arrival from Germany in the quaint and picturesque costume of their country".

19th CENTURY METHODIST CHURCH, DEMOLISHED 1966

The Methodist Church at Combermere, Radcliffe Township, on the banks of the Madawaska River was demolished in 1966 and had not been used as a place of worship since 1928 when the Methodist Synod sold it. The associated cemetery is maintained in perpetuity in memory of the people who settled the community. In the 1881 census of Raglan and Radcliffe Townships families who declared their allegiance to the Methodist denomination included: Bergur, Limerand, Kurtguey, Niewman, Ewit, Thom, Kapakaski, Gransey, Schroider, Frantz, Budarick, Musclow, Haiss, Brown, Walters, Schutt, Groshles, Wasmond, Phitzner, Griese, Pfannenhour, Boehme, Seafield, Towns, Denzion and Boubrie, all except the last-named being immigrants from Germany. The Methodist minister was an Irishman, Andrew Wilson. It was the difficulty of supplying German-speaking ministers that caused the Methodist Church to withdraw from its German Missions in eastern Ontario in favour of the Evangelical Association in 1883. At this church, built in the 1870s, Methodist services were apparently discontinued in the 1890s when an Anglican church was built in the village of Combermere.

Photograph reproduced courtesy Nelson Boehme, Combermere.

This account suggests that the reporter did not interview anybody, but merely observed at a distance.

Although the German presence had not occupied much space in the local weekly newspapers, their numbers had made the creation of new post offices necessary in the rural townships. One of the earliest ones to be staffed by a German immigrant who could translate letters (if necessary) for those who could not write or read in any language was on the Ottawa and Opeongo Colonization Road, in Sebastopol Township. Albert Kosmack, who had first settled in Lyndoch Township and then purchased a farm in Sebastopol Township, was the postmaster who conducted the post office business from his residence. It is believed that he chose the name *Vanbrugh* from a painting on the wall — and it does not

A second German post office was opened in Sebastopol Township, following the arrival of Mrs. Gottlieb Woermke, a widow who came to Canada with nine children soon after her second husband's death in 1882. Mrs. Gottlieb was made postmistress and she named the office *Woermke*. In Alice Township, the postmaster who headed a family with the surname of Woito, called the community just that, *Woito*. In Raglan Township, where later German immigrants settled, a post office was established, with Christie F. Schutt as postmaster, and once again the family name christened the small community, *Schutt*.

At the junction of Raglan, Radcliffe and Brudenell Townships, another German place name appeared in a community of more modest size, *Rosenthal*, the first postmaster being Charles (or Carl) Phanenhaur. Wesley Budd, the third generation of a German-Canadian family to inhabit the farmhouse at Budd Mills, Wilberforce Township, which included a post office on the premises, can remember what a social centre it used to be. Area residents, anxious for mail or for the latest copy of a German language newspaper, would sit down and read.

The German immigrants who settled in Renfrew County and just beyond its borders have contributed far fewer place names than their relative numbers would indicate. Many moved into villages that had once been occupied by Irish immigrants in earlier years, such as Letterkenny, Maynooth or Donegal; the areas had been surveyed before they arrived and the language of the surveyors and commerce was English or French. Rankin, Locksley and Golden Lake became the enclaves of German immigrants. In one case, *Quadeville*, this community in Lyndoch Township, was originally named Strathtay, but a long established German family founded by August Quade requested a name change in 1908.

19th CENTURY LUTHERAN CHURCH
The congregation of St. John's Lutheran Church of the Missouri Synod in Germanicus was organized in 1872 and held services in a public school, S.S. No. 8 Wilberforce Township. In 1878 this church was built of logs, 42' by 30', followed in 1882 by a church school where the children were taught catechism and academic subjects in the German language. The church was clapboarded in 1890. By the turn of the century there were at least 50 churches in Eastern Ontario where worship was conducted in the German language, many of them "little white churches" such as this one. St. John's congregation at Germanicus constructed a new church of red brick in 1923 and the old church was demolished. The use of the German language was gradually phased out in the church services, in the years between the two world wars, and now is only used at an occasional Christmas or anniversary service.
Photograph by Martha Schiemann. Reproduced courtesy Mrs. Paul Panke.

CENTURY FARM THAT HOSTED THE PREACHER
In this one-and-a-half storey farmhouse that was begun in 1868 by a stonemason from Silesia, Gustave Michel, and finished by 1872, the bedroom on the right side of the upper floor was maintained for the use of the Lutheran pastor. Before the congregation of St. John's, on the Black Bay Road, Petawawa Township, built its first log church in 1875, services were held in the Michel home. In the last quarter of the 19th century, the congregation here was too small to support a resident pastor and it relied on the visits of clergymen from other Lutheran churches. In the home of the Michels, a room named the *prophenstube* was set aside exclusively for this visitor, a common practice in German Lutheran parishes that were spread over large areas. Church records show that in 1878-79 Gustave Michel was paid $8 for hosting the pastor every three weeks; in 1885, he received 50 cents a year from each member of the congregation for the boarding of the pastor every two weeks.
When this log farmhouse was cleared out following the death of Oscar Michel, in 1981, a handwritten copy of the constitution of St. John's Lutheran Church's congregation was found.

have a German connotation. In Wilberforce Township, where the area north-west of Lake Dore had become densely settled by German immigrants, the post office was given the contrived name of *Germanicus*. At the intersection of Grattan and South Algona Townships, where there was another close community of German immigrants who called the place *Augsburg*, a post office was established in the home of John Wodtke and his wife in 1878.

THE BUCKWALDS BECAME A

Mr. and Mrs. Ferdinand Buckwald (se
Canada from Germany c. 1881, and settle(.
with their family at a time when there w(.
church in that area. Like several other Germar.
Buckwalds joined the Anglican church in Eg
John the Evangelist. They were photographe(.
village, c. 1890 by J.A. Smith, with their three c.
Gustave, Henrietta (Mrs. Edward Zadow) and Otto.
descendants of Gustave Buckwald remained members o.
John's church and served as wardens.

Photograph reproduced courtesy Mrs. Norman Zadow.

SHE BOARDED THE PREACHER

Survivor of a long voyage on a sailing ship, which claimed the lives of two daughters and a son, Caroline (nee Fritsch) Michel, the wife of Gustave Michel, arrived childless in Petawawa Township in 1867. Aged 35 when she reached her new country, Caroline gave birth to three more sons, Robert (1868), Bruno (1872) and Emil (1875). Mrs. Michel's spacious log home on the Black Bay Road (see previous photograph) was the scene of early services of St. John's Lutheran Church; for a quarter of a century this house, and this housewife, boarded the visiting ministers. After her husband's death in 1892, Caroline Michel was photographed in Pembroke in her widow's weeds. She died April 25, 1909.

Photograph reproducted courtesy Mrs. Martha Ragelis, Petawawa Township.

LOG CHURCH OF LUTHERAN PIONEERS
The first Lutheran services in the community of German farmers in Sebastopol Township were conducted in 1863 by Rev. L.H. Gerndt, a missionary. In subsequent years the community was visited by Methodists, Baptists and preachers from the Evangelical Association. Not until 1873 did a second Lutheran missionary conduct services here on the Ottawa and Opeongo Colonization Road. The congregation grew to such a size that the members felt that they could support a church building, and in 1890 the site was purchased and the logs assembled. The contractors for the building were Messrs. Fred and George Morlock. These men were assisted by members of the congregation, such as: Carl Musclow, Richard Schweigert, William Hildebrandt, August Seller, Edward Ziebarth, William Schmidt, Christian Heideman, Ferdinand Zoschke, Albert Kosmack, Rheinhold Rose, Karl Rosien and William Schroeder. This church building was dedicated on August 17, 1890. Changed over the years by the addition of a belfry tower and white board siding, the church at Vanbrugh, St. John's Lutheran, was in regular use until the early 1970s. When it was closed and threatened with demolition, it was saved from destruction by 10 parishioners who raised the money to buy it in 1978. It is used occasionally.

Photograph reproduced courtesy Allan Kosmack, Vanbrugh.

COMMUNION CLOTH FROM EVANGELICAL CHURCH
A border on three sides of this communion table cloth was crocheted by a member of the Evangelical Church at Golden Lake in 1894. Descendants donated it to the Champlain Trail Museum at Pembroke. In many of the German churches, in the first and second generations of the congregation, it was customary for the women to sit on one side of the nave and the men on the other. The front of this cloth bears the inscription "Ich bin das Broddes Lebens", which means "I am the Bread of Life". On the left-hand side, where it could be seen by the female communicants, the border has a design of vine leaves. On the right-hand side of the cloth, where it could be seen by the men, the border has an inscription "Prufe dich Selblt!". This message, which translates as "Examine thyself!" is believed to have been a rebuke to the men whose behaviour might provide grounds for suspicion.

PULPIT MADE OF PINE
St. John's Lutheran Church of the Canada Synod at Vanbrugh, Sebastopol Township, is a log church that has kept some of its original furnishings. A German immigrant, Fred Morlock, made this pulpit and the altar from pine in 1890. Although he lived in Eganville, Mr. Morlock earned his living principally as a wood-carver on the interiors of churches in Quebec — which explains the fleur-de-lys motif. This pulpit, the altar, the lectern and the 1887 organ (which has mouse-proof pedals) were all grain-painted at the time of the congregation's 100th anniversary in 1963. Saved from demolition by ten families who raised the purchase price of $2500 in 1978, the church is used only for special occasions and the floor is sprinkled with mothballs to deter wildlife which might enter from the bush surrounding the building.

WOODEN GRAVE MARKER
Simple wooden crosses, which do not last as long as stone memorials, were used to mark many burial places in the 19th century and have since disappeared. Any record of surnames made from extant grave markers is therefore incomplete.

A few wooden crosses are still found in some of the cemeteries in the rural townships of eastern Ontario. This one, bearing an inscription in the German language, was photographed in 1974 in the cemetery of St. John's Lutheran Church, Black Bay Road, Petawawa Township, and bears no date.

PIONEER CHURCH IN HASTINGS COUNTY
This Emmanuel Methodist Church was built 1880 - 1882 at Maynooth, Hastings County. It is surrounded by the gravestones of pioneers who settled on the Peterson Road, a thoroughfare which connected the Hastings Colonization Road with the Ottawa and Opeongo Colonization Road — both routes which had been advertised in Germany. The earliest settlers in this area were British, the Irish naming the community Doyle's Corners before the title Maynooth was bestowed on it. Surnames of German pioneers on the gravestones around this church include: Musclow, Brose, Lebow, Wasmund, Fiss, Bahm, Mickael, Hienz, Hinz, Wolkenstein, Frantz, Zeise, Brandenberg, Gieser, Geiser, Popp and Maschke. According to Hastings County historian, Mrs. Jean Richter, the church was used by Methodists and Anglicans, later Methodists and Presbyterians, and joined the United Church of Canada in the 1920's. Known locally as "the white church", its cemetery was still used for burials in 1980, although there had not been any regular worship in the church for years.

FROM WEST PRUSSIA
The immigration agent who worked in Germany for the Canadian government, 1860 - 1862, anticipated that the states in eastern Germany might be the most likely source of people who wished to own land. Wrote William Wagner, "Those emigrants chiefly fit for our climate and for clearing the Canadian woods are those who are living in the eastern part of Germany, that is to say in quarters which have only been cleared during the last century, or to name them more particularly, the Provinces of West Prussia, Pomerania, Posen, Silesia, and the eastern part of Brandenburg."

This gravestone at Augsburg marks the burial place of Ferdinand E. Kant who was born in West Prussia. Following the war of 1870-71, Mr. Kant and his bride, Wilhelmina Byers, emigrated to Canada, settling on a grant of land in South Algona Township. Three of their sons were among the group of German farmers in Renfrew County who tried to establish another German-speaking settlement on the Canadian Shield, near Englehart, in the years before the First World War.

VANBRUGH POST OFFICE

On adjoining lots on the Ottawa and Opeongo Colonization Road in Sebastopol Township, a group of well-educated German immigrants purchased farms from Free Grant settlers in the 1860s. In 1865 four of them signed a letter addressed to a Canadian immigration agent, W.J. Wills assuring him of the progress and success of their community which became known as VANBRUGH, taking its name from the post office. Albert Kosmack, who lived in this house and conducted the post office business from his residence, is believed to have chosen the name from a painting that was hanging in his home. This structure was inhabited by three successive generations of Kosmacks until 1935 and it was demolished in 1980.

WOERMKE POST OFFICE

When the four German farmers at Vanbrugh wrote a letter to W.J. Wills in 1865, informing him of their progress, they also suggested that the hilly land south of their community should be developed. "At the back of our settlement there is a large tract of land, very capable of being worked and which would be opened up by a road. The eventual settlers on this land would be very much assisted by Mr. A. Kosmack, who gives every advice and assistance to those settling in his neighbourhood and who has made a good winter road through this tract of land". To this part of Sebastopol Township, Mrs. Gottlieb Woermke, a widow from Germany with nine children, came in 1882, and from this home ran the post office, which she named after her family.

VANBRUGH POST OFFICE 1894

Pictured by a Denbigh photographer in 1894 in front of their home on the Ottawa and Opeongo Road are the German immigrants Albert Kosmack (1842-1924) (with folded arms) and his buxom wife, Whilhelmina Quade, with some of their daughters, standing before a field of fine cabbages. The couple had eleven children altogether. The name VANBRUGH can be seen on the side of the building, which served as a post office for the residents of the area. Grandson Allan Kosmack recalled that people would travel several miles to collect their mail here, and his grandfather, Albert Kosmack, postmaster for 48 years, wrote letters for some who were illiterate. The farmhouse was eventually transferred to a son, Frederick Kosmack (1879-1962) who was married to Adeline Gierman, and later, Mr. and Mrs. Allan Kosmack owned it.

Photograph reproduced courtesy Allan Kosmack.

Chapter II.

Settling in a new country

By 1881 the numbers of German people in Renfrew County had more than doubled in ten years, from 2,318 in 1871 to 4,831. There were only 478 living in the two villages and one town — Arnprior, 131, Renfrew, 219, and in the town of Pembroke, 128 — the remainder had located in the townships. Though Wilberforce and Alice still had the largest numbers, by now the German immigrants had begun to spread to the western townships, as the following figures show: Admaston Twp., 148; Alice and Fraser Twps., 736; Bagot and Blythfield Twps., 19; Bromley Twp., 44; Brougham, 0; Brudenell and Lynedock (sic) Twps., 180; Grattan Twp., 126; Head, Clara and Maria Twps., 27; Horton Twp., 12; McNab Twp., 204; Matawatchan and Griffith Twps., 3; Pembroke Twp., 1; Petawawa and McKay Twps., 247; Raglan and Radcliffe Twps., 282; Ross Twp., 28; Sebastopol Twp., 189; South Algona Twp., 199; Stafford Twp., 85; Westmeath Twp., 62; Wilberforce and North Algona Twps., 987.

Much of the increase was due to the birth rate. For example, Matthew Horcun and his wife, who had arrived in 1863 with three children, had eight offspring by 1881. The majority of immigrants who came in the 1860s were young adults and they had large families. Census records also show that after the couple had been in Canada a few years they were joined by elderly parents, sometimes widowed, whose age would preclude them from vigorous work. Persons over the age of 60 years were not accepted by the German sailing vessels appointed for the travel of immigrants to the U.S.A., even if accompanied by a son capable of earning a living. The regulations enforced by the City of Hamburg and the Royal Prussian Ministry for business and trade would only allow the passage of persons who were physically and mentally sound. Anyone suspected of infectious disease, frailty or filthiness would be refused entry to the ship. Others that were not allowed on board included persons who were deaf or mute, the mentally retarded, blind people, cripples, widows, unaccompanied women with children and pregnant women who were travelling alone. The provisions were clearly intended to ensure that fit and healthy immigrants arrived at the end of the journey, if they survived the ocean crossing. They would need all their strength for the arduous work ahead.

If any elderly parents wished to accompany or join their family in Canada, they were allowed to enter by a Canadian port. Any indepth immigration study of the German settlement in Renfrew County would find it impossible to assess the number of arrivals by studying the records of ships that docked at Halifax or Quebec. Many families arrived at New York, with some members travelling on to Canada and others staying in the United States. Conversely, there were those who came to Canada, journeyed to Renfrew County and after a short stay decided to travel south to the United States.

By whichever route they made their way to Renfrew County, the family groups tended to stay close together, with brothers and cousins, fathers and adult sons settling in the same township, often side by side. The lack of communication between German-speaking immigrants and their British neighbours was a drawback noted by an immigration agent of the Canadian government, William Sinn, in October 1860, when he visited 50 German farms in the townships of Admaston, Alice, North and South Algona, Bromley and Wilberforce, as well as three on the Ottawa and Opeongo Colonization Road. The harvest had been larger than usual that year, the average yield of wheat estimated at more than 30 bushels per acre, and the new settlers had expressed their satisfaction at the choice of a district where they could possess a homestead and expect to achieve independence. Mr. Sinn's calculations of their crops and records of their livestock were designed to assure those in Germany, who were contemplating a move to Canada, especially to the Ottawa district, that the prospects were good.

Though the promise seemed bright, most of the land on the Canadian Shield in Renfrew County was poor for agriculture, the thin soil hidden by dense forest. This was the countryside that was described in glowing terms in the brochures that were offered (in the German language) by Canadian government agents who hoped to recruit immigrants from Germany. The overriding temptation to move to new countries such as Australia, the United States or Canada was provided by the large expanses of unoccupied land. In a country such as Germany, where over-population threatened poverty for many, where farmers saw their holdings dwindle in size or disappear altogether, the offer of free land or cheap

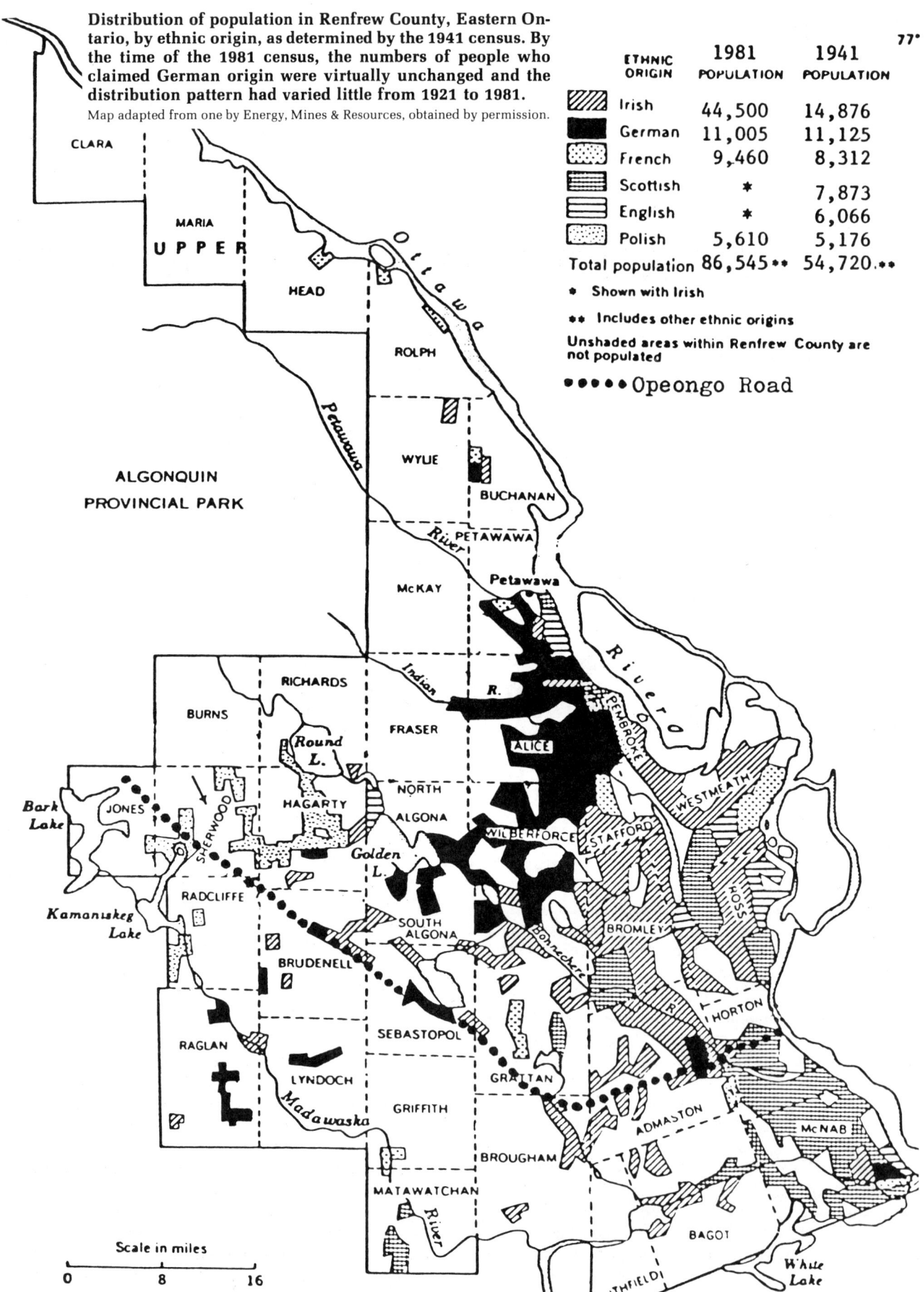

land was irresistible. In 1855, the Commissioner of Crown Lands in Canada, the Hon. Peter Vankoughnet committed the government to a policy of settlement in the Ottawa-Huron region by means of free grants of land along colonization roads; these were meant to encourage immigration from overseas and to expand a new agricultural region in Canada West.

At first the advertisements were circulated in the British Isles only, together with 12,000 copies of a 24-page pamphlet that described the Ottawa and Opeongo Road, the Addington and the Hastings Roads, the first three roads where free land was offered. Translations into German (6,000), Norwegian (5,000) and French (4,000) were sent to the continent in order to make Canada better known in Europe. Posters advised prospective immigrants of the best route to take and how to find the office of the Crown Lands Agent who would supervise settlement on the colonization road. All three roads attracted immigrants from Germany, and Otto von Bismarck himself remarked that one of the chief inducements for Germans to leave their country were the persuasive letters that came from other family members contentedly settled overseas.

Bismarck's ambition was considered by many to be sufficient reason to leave Germany, for the wars of 1863, 1867 and the final one of 1870-71 that united the country, had caused uneasiness among the population. Oddly enough, some of the German immigrants who landed at New York in the early 1860s realised that they could earn money by joining the Union Army that was then engaged in a civil war. After they had been discharged from the service, the young men either stayed in the United States or travelled north to Canada. If they had been wounded in wartime service they were eligible for a pension; if they died from natural causes, their widows could claim a pension. Some did.

Though all three colonization roads offered free grants to settlers in eastern Ontario, the Ottawa and Opeongo Road was the one that attracted the largest numbers of German people. It had been promoted, in glowing terms, in a pamphlet written by the Crown Lands Agent on that road, T.P. French, who was no doubt prompted by self-interest. As he wrote in his brochure, the value of land is regulated by the principles of supply and demand, and Canada, with its immense territory and comparatively thin population, could make an offer which was impossible in those countries which had small size and numerous inhabitants. He warned the intending immigrant to ponder seriously on the chances of success in a new environment "before relinquishing his pursuits at home, disturbing his domestic arrangements, and entering on a long and expensive journey, that may, possibly, result in blighted expectations, and a subsequent life of unavailing sorrow". Having delivered this admonishment, Mr. French proceeded to paint an optimistic picture of success.

AGENCY FOR THE SETTLEMENT
OF THE
HASTINGS ROAD

July, 1856.

THE undersigned, Agent appointed by His Excellency the Governor General for the Settlement of the Hastings Road, in the rear of the County of Hastings, Upper Canada, hereby gives notice to all persons willing and having the means of locating thereon, that his office is (for the present) in the Township of Madoc, and which will be open every day in the week, between the hours of Nine and Four o'clock.

One Hundred Acres will be given to any settler eighteen years old, and a subject of Her Majesty, who will present himself provided with a certificate of probity and sobriety signed by known and respectable persons, and having the means of providing for himself until the produce of his land is sufficient to maintain him. The bearer of that certificate shall mention to the Agent (who shall keep a registry thereof) his name, age, condition, trade or profession; whether he is married, and if so the name and age of his wife; how many children he has, the name and age of each of them; where he is from, and whether he is the owner of land elsewhere.

The conditions of location are, to take possession within a month, and to put in a state of cultivation at least twelve acres of the land in the course of four years,—to build a house (at least 20 by 18 feet) and to reside on the lot until the conditions of settlement are duly performed; after which accomplishment only shall the settler have the right of obtaining a title of property. Families comprising several settlers entitled to lands, preferring to reside on a single lot, will be exempted from the obligation of building and of residence (except upon the lot on which they live) provided that the required clearing of the land be made on each lot. The non-accomplishment of these conditions will cause the immediate loss of the assigned lot of land, which will be sold or given to another.

The Road having been opened by the Government, the settlers are required to keep it in repair.

The nearest Lake Port to the Agency is Belleville.

M. P. HAYES,
Agent, Hastings Road.

HASTINGS ROAD

The 74-mile long Hastings Road, from Madoc to Bancroft (sometimes called Hastings) was opened up for settlement in 1856. In a pamphlet made available to emigrants in Germany, the Crown Lands Agent, M.P. Hayes, advised that the direct way to reach the Hastings Road was by way of Kingston, Canada West, thence by steamboat up the Bay of Quinte to Belleville 56 miles. Comparatively few German immigrants chose this road, but those that did settle on it journeyed to the end of the road, where it intersected with the Peterson Road, and founded a German-speaking community at Maynooth.

Poster reproduced from the Ontario Archives. R.G. 1., A-1-7, Box 13.

HER HUSBAND SERVED IN THE AMERICAN CIVIL WAR

Born Dec. 4, 1848, in Lubnau Konitz, Pomerania, Caroline Wilhelmine Schwarz was the daughter of Carl and Wilhelmina Schwarz with whom she emigrated in 1858 to Canada, settling first at Fitzroy Harbor. She married Johann Wilhelm (William) Gorr, Oct. 28, 1869, a German immigrant who had served in the Civil War in the United States before clearing land in Alice Township for a farm which is still in the possession of descendants. William died Dec. 10, 1884, at the age of 44, as a result of heart failure while building a barn. His widow, who had just given birth to her sixth child a few weeks earlier, applied to the American government for a pension because her husband was a war veteran, having been honorably discharged from the New York State volunteers, Sept. 1, 1865. With the aid of this pension and the help of her four sons, she kept the farm going. Caroline died Dec. 31, 1924.

Photograph reproduced courtesy Robbie Gorr, Pembroke.

FOUR SONS WHO ESCAPED ARMY SERVICE

Johann and Ernestine Luloff left Germany in 1867 because they had four young sons, aged from two to 11 years old, and the parents wanted to be sure that their boys would not be obliged to enter military service. Having grown up in Canada on a farm in North Algona Township, the four sons posed for this photograph with their mother. Back row, left to right, are Ferdinand (1856-1934), Wilhelm (1859-1939) and Herman (1861-1943); sitting beside his mother (1830-1914) is Edward (1865-1946).

Photograph reproduced courtesy Miss Teresa Luloff, Golden Lake.

He wrote, "All kinds of cereals, vegetables and fruits grow well, and by the man who is capable of doing his own farming they can be produced at comparatively little cost, and to him they are sure to yield a profitable return for his labor. But, as in all new countries, labor is scarce, and consequently expensive, he who is incapable of taking the axe, the plough, the scythe and sickle, in his own hand, and using them effectively, cannot hope to realize much profit from pursuits exclusively agricultural. There are many other avocations, however, to which a man with a small capital may usefully turn; and as the *Dignity of Labour* is here fully recognized, the particular nature of his employment will be in nowise affect his respectability, provided he be always found honest in his dealings, and moral in his conduct."

After describing the wages of a working man and that of servant girls, Mr. French listed shoemakers, tailors, blacksmiths and carpenters as being the tradesmen most in demand in the newer parts of Canada. He thought that masons would also find work in the large towns and cities. His advice may have been influential, for those trades were well represented among the German immigrants who came to eastern Ontario, although they were in the minority; most of the newcomers were drawn by the prospect of land, even if they had to earn the money at some other occupation in order to make payments on a property.

Although Mr. French mentioned that the lumber shanties in the Ottawa Valley would be a certain and profitable market for the surplus produce of the farms, especially beef, pork, flour, potatoes, peas, oats and hay, he did not suggest that these same lumber shanties might be a source of employment for skilled and unskilled labor. There is hardly a long-established family in the Ottawa Valley which does not have a store of photographs taken at a lumber camp where one of their relatives once worked. The associated industries, such as sawmills, tool manufacturers and axe factories were also places where immigrants might find work, as a temporary measure, while saving money to buy a piece of land. Working in the woods in wintertime, when much of the farm work is suspended because of the blanket of snow that covers the ground, was an addition to the family's income that was common until the years of the second world war.

The severity of the Canadian winter was lightly touched on in the brochure for intending immigrants to the Ottawa Valley. "In this section of the Province sleighing can rarely be calculated on with any degree of certainty before Christmas in each year, and it ends about the 10th April," was one of the casual references that the Crown Lands Agent permitted himself. He was similarly optimistic about the ease with which a newcomer could construct a dwelling, declaring that neighbours would offer prompt gratuitous assistance for the construction of a shanty which could be built by 12 men in one day. According to Mr. French, "The best possible feeling prevails among the Settlers, and no kindness that anyone of them can render is ever denied to the stranger, no matter from what country he hails, or at what altar he kneels". Occasionally that first small dwelling might be offered to other newly-arrived immigrants on a temporary basis. Such generosity was probably harmonious and little-recorded, the exception being one that made headlines and resulted in Renfrew County's second hanging.

"The second execution was in 1887, the murderer being a German settler in Raglan Township named "X"* who admitted the brutal murder of a woman near his home. "X" had come out from the old country and settling in Raglan, had through industry and thrift prospered in his home. On his arrival he built a rude cabin to live in, but as conditions improved he built a more substantial house a short distance away. Former friends in Germany wrote him, suggesting that they come to Canada, and he urged them to do so, offering them the use of his old

DESCENDANTS OF THE QUAST THAT STAYED
Well-dressed, looking hale and hearty, Frederick Quast posed with his wife and two of their ten children, John and Alma, in Eganville, a village to which a Pembroke photographer made occasional visits.
Frederick had been only four years old when his father Gotlieb Quast, emigrated from Breitenstein, Kreis Friedeberg, Frankfurt-on-the-Oder in 1860. Gotlieb and his brother, Christian Quast, headed two of the six families who left the same village that summer to travel to Eastern Ontario, specifically to South Algona Township, at the urging of Wilhelm Schroder who had made the journey a year earlier. Christian Quast is believed to have moved to the United States after a short stay in Renfrew County, but Gotlieb Quast remained. One of Gotlieb's five sons had eighteen children, but there is only one descendant of this surname still farming in South Algona Township in 1986. Wilbert Quast, who has expanded his acreage by the purchase of several farms.
Photograph reproduced courtesy Ferdinand Kant, Iroquois Falls

cabin until they could establish themselves.

"The new settlers obtained land some distance away, but lived in "X"'s cabin even after they had cleared considerable land and were in a position to build a house of their own, remaining until they apparently became obsessed with the idea that "X" was powerless to evict them. Efforts on his part to get rid of his unwelcome and non-paying tenants were fruitless and eventually he served an ultimatum that unless they moved the following day he would put them out. The following morning he returned to the cabin. The man had gone to his own farm, leaving his wife and children in the cabin and she told "X" that they were not going to leave. He then got hammer and nails and nailed up the door, with the people inside, and set fire to the building.

* The name of the murderer has been omitted from this contemporary newspaper account because there are residents in Renfrew County who bear this surname.

SCOOP ROOF ON LOG SHANTY
Made of logs that had not been squared, a shanty was a hastily constructed dwelling that served to house pioneer settlers during their first winter. The roof was made of split and hollowed-out logs, laid in a concave-convex arrangement that carried off the rainfall. This shanty is located on the Ottawa and Opeongo Road in Sebastopol Township, where Gottlieb Gierman and his two sons from Germany purchased a farm from an Irish family in 1870, after working for three years in the logging industry in Renfrew. These immigrants from Prenzlau moved into a community which had been named Clontarf by earlier Irish settlers who took up Free Grants of land. This shanty was the Giermans' first home before they built a two-storey house of squared logs with dovetailed corners.

FIRST HOUSE, LONG ABANDONED
On a road in Alice Township that leads to Pembroke, this one-and-a-half-storey log house was the home of John and Johanna Teske, from Germany, who were 68 and 76 by the time of 1881 census, and one of the few Roman Catholic couples in the township. Local residents believe that this old dwelling, boarded-up and unoccupied, was an original homestead of pioneers.

"The woman had an axe and with this she succeeded in battering down the door, after which she sent the children out of the burning building and prepared to follow him. "X" in the meantime had armed himself with an ironwood sleighstake, and as she came out of the door he struck her a terrible blow over the head. The woman fell in front of the door and as the cabin was consumed in flames her head and the upper portion of her body was burned to cinders".

The murderer surrendered to police the next day and offered no defence at his trial in Pembroke, where he appeared thoroughly repentant. Although the incident was provoked by newcomers who abused hospitality, the dispute and the violence contradict the impression that pioneering years were times of gentle neighbourliness.

One writer who has documented the settlement of German people from Pennsylvania into southern Ontario, noted the different lifestyles of those who moved from Germany to the Ottawa Valley.

G. Elmore Reaman in his book, The Trail of the Black Walnut, wrote "The fact that settlers in eastern Ontario migrated in large numbers at the same time, locating in contiguous areas, tended to give them a solidarity and also a hold on the government not possessed by settlers who had come in as individuals. In many cases, however, they had not had very much experience in pioneering, consequently they were not quite as successful as the German farmers from Pennsylvania. They built their log cabins differently, for instead of putting the fireplace in the centre of the building they put it at one end. Nor did they build large barns, partly because of the lack of sawmills".

Water-powered sawmills were indeed few in the townships where the German people had settled, but there was no shortage of wood. Whether logs were hastily assembled for a shanty or more carefully squared and dovetailed for a more sturdy structure, the homes built by the German immigrants were essentially the same as those constructed by other settlers in Renfrew County who had arrived earlier in the 19th century. In some cases, the newcomers from Germany purchased farms that had already been cleared and had dwellings erected on them. Small log houses might be supplanted by large log houses as progress was made. In time, large log houses might be covered with boards or brick siding to improve their appearance. Those farmers who lived within easy access of a brickyard, either by road or railway track, might eventually replace their wooden house by a brick structure. Those who lived within easy distance of a sawmill, and steam-powered sawmills became more numerous in the last decade of the 19th century, would build later barns with sawn timber instead of logs. But little was discarded. A typical German farm in Renfrew County consists of a collection of wooden buildings of different dates. The house may have been improved, but the sheds and barns that housed livestock, crops and farm machinery are a mixture of logs and sawn timber, unpainted and without any embellishment. There are no hex signs or painted scenes

FIRST HOUSE USED FOR LIVESTOCK

The first log house that was built might be small and eventually outgrown, but on some farms it has been retained and used for other purposes. The first log house built by William Fick was a single-storey dwelling with a central chimney and it now serves as a henhouse on the property occupied by the third and fourth generation, the principal change being a new roof. A farmer, William Fick, and his wife, Fredericka, 50, were listed in the 1871 census, together with two adult sons who were carpenters, Gustave, 26, and William 22, and a daughter, Whilimine, 24, living at home.

to distinguish these German farms. Quite often the first house of the immigrants may have been converted to use as a henhouse or pig-sty.

At the scene of its reconstruction on the museum grounds at Pembroke, the Chusroskie farmhouse built by German immigrants has been supplied with a well, the sort of well that was provided by excavating a hole in the ground, lining it with stone, and hauling up the water in buckets. A depth of six feet was usually enough to reach water. Though most of these early wells were covered with a lid, for reasons of safety, they were a constant hazard, judging from contemporary accounts in old newspapers and family histories. One who lost his wife in this was August Kruger, the founder, in 1905, of another German-speaking community in northern Ontario. On a day when Mr. Kruger had gone to visit a neighbour in Germanicus, to enquire about the time of the funeral for Wilhelmine Lipke, the first wife of Johann Gotlieb Lipke, who died Feb. 17, 1881, he returned home to discover that he too had been widowed. His wife had fallen down the well. More often it was curious children who drowned in this way. The use of pumps removed this danger.

The early water pumps were constructed almost entirely of wood. The pipe was made by boring out the centre of a log, usually from the tamarack tree, and the shaft consisted of a long pole to which a handle was attached at the top end. The commonest type of piston was a wooden cylinder, fringed with leather, which fitted inside the pipe and which acted as a "sucker". Pumping the handle up and down caused the shaft to raise and lower the piston, and this repeated suction brought a column of water to the surface.

SCOTTISH AND GERMAN HOUSES WERE ALIKE

The log house photographed c. 1878 (above) was occupied by the Scottish family of Peter McDonald and was built in 1857 on lot 30, con. 8, Admaston Township, Renfrew County, by Charles Bowes, John Smith and others.
Photo Ontario Archives.

Log houses of identical design were constructed by many German immigrants, such as this home in Wilberforce Township, Renfrew County, (below) which was built by William Wolfgram in 1877 and is occupied by his descendants.

25

In Petawawa Township, when Paul Schwanz retired from farming in 1974, his vegetable garden was still watered with the aid of a tamarack sucker pump; the "sucker" occasionally had to be replaced and Mr. Schwanz produced an old one to show how it was made.

In Wilberforce Township, a wooden sucker pump still produces water for the cattle trough in the centre of a barnyard on the farm of Wesley Fick.

Iron pumps were introduced in the middle of the 19th century and gradually supplanted the wooden pump on most farms, although some farmers preferred the tamarack pump because its wider bore produced a greater volume of water. Oscar Michel, who was the third generation of his family to occupy a farm in Petawawa Township, remembered that his father, Robert Michel, changed from a wooden pump to an iron pump before the first world war and then changed back again to a wooden pump for this reason. A maker of wooden pumps, Albert Schultz, was still active in the Pembroke-Petawawa area well into the 1920s, and the results of his work are still to be found on some of the German farms in Renfrew County, some pumps covered and some pumps exposed to the elements. The iron pump needed no protection from the weather, but the wooden pump would last longer if it was housed in a shed that was built just large enough to contain both the pump and the operator. Those wooden pumps that were covered have remained in good condition, although the "sucker" has to be replaced at intervals. In those that are not covered, the wood will deteriorate in time and a replacement for the hollow log is needed. In 1977, the National Museum of Science and Technology displayed a pump-boring machine at the annual Steam Engine Show at Petawawa the work of drilling out the hole being performed by a gasoline engine. The hollowed-out logs were much appreciated by some local farmers who quietly spirited them away.

WOODEN PUMP
Banded with metal, this hollowed-out tamarack sucker pump once served as a source of water for livestock in the barnyard of a farm in Petawawa Township, owned by the descendants of Ferdinand Goldt, an immigrant from Germany. In a nearby cemetery of Christ Lutheran church (of the Missouri Synod) the gravestone of Carl Goldt (1840-1905) records that his birthplace was at Kreis Plato, in Deutchland.

OLD LOG HOUSE NEAR AN AIRPORT
This is the second log house on this property built by Freidrich B. Burgomeister, one of the earliest German immigrants to settle in Petawawa Township. There were only nine listed on the assessment rolls of 1867, by which year Burgomeister's farm already had cattle, sheep, a hog, a horse and six persons in the family, the oldest born in Ontario in 1861. The Burgomeister family left this property on con. one, lot 22, in 1892, but the building appears to have been little altered despite several owners and its proximity to the Pembroke and Area Airport.

IRISH LOG HOUSE OCCUPIED BY GERMAN FAMILY
When the Zadow family of widowed mother and four sons emigrated to Canada in 1881, this log farmhouse was purchased by the mother, Charlotte Auguste Kreuger Zadow Zillmer, from an Irish family named O'Keefe in South Algona Township. The building housed the mother and the growing family of her son, Edward; later, the family of Edward's son, August, lived there with nine children, and finally a member of the third generation, Driscoll, made it his home. The structure was still sturdy when the last Zadow left it in 1979 after 98 years of living there.

In 1881, when the Zadows arrived, the Irish residents in South Algona Township totalled 405 and the Germans numbered 199. The Irish were gradually replaced as the majority in this township by the influx of German immigrants. Forty years later, the Irish numbered 234, while the Germans had increased to 418.

AMBITIOUS STRUCTURE
Nov. 1977. Constructed by Martin Kruger, who was born July 7, 1827, at Schonhohe, Kottbus, Germany, this finely-built log farmhouse covered by board and batten, Wilberforce Township, remained unchanged for three generations of the Krugers. The last owner died without relatives in 1975. While he was in hospital, the entire contents of the house were looted.

FARM BUILDINGS MADE OF LOGS
Timber was so abundant that round or squared logs were used in the construction of farm buildings. The well-stocked woodshed was on the farm of John Luloff in Grattan Township; the henhouse was built by Bill Berndt on a Wilberforce Township farm originally cleared by the Manteufels.

July 1978. Careful demolition of the Kruger farmhouse by a new owner who purchased the building in order to construct log home on a waterfront site on the Ottawa River. In the distance is the Woito Evangelical Lutheran church, to which the Krugers donated land and money. Rear view of house shows a summer kitchen.

ARRANGEMENT OF FARM BUILDINGS
The one-and-a-half storey 'vernacular house of Ontario' facing the road and the collection of large and small log buildings that are spaced around a square yard represent the toil of more than a century of farming this inhospitable land. Julius Remus emigrated from Plagow, Kreis Arnswalde, in 1870 and met Fredericka Becker from Falkenstein, Kreis Freidenburg on the ocean crossing. The couple married in Canada and settled on land in Lyndoch Township in 1875. Their first log dwelling has long since disappeared. Descendants are still working the farm.

Mr. and Mrs. Fred Thur posed c. 1915 in front of their log farmhouse which has been covered by bricks. This couple, who married Sept. 3, 1885, purchased the farmhouse from an Irish family named Madigan; it was close to their parents' homes at Golden Lake where they had been born in 1861 and 1862 respectively. A neighbour, Wesley Budd, could remember the arrival of the bricks from Pembroke when he was a child, about 1900, at the site of the Thurs' home on lot 23, con. 17, Wilberforce Township.
Covering the exterior of a log house with bricks (or the building of a new home from bricks) was an option available only to those with access to brickyards by rail or by good roads. Until 1934 road communications in the western townships of Renfrew County were poor, but Golden Lake was served by a railroad spur from Pembroke.

Photograph reproduced courtesy Golden Lake Women's Institute.

CONSTRUCTING A BRICK HOUSE. 1909-1910
In Alice Township, where good land and close proximity to markets helped to make small farms successful, brick houses replaced some of the log dwellings in the early years of the 20th century. (Some schools and churches were built of brick then as well, for it was a comparatively prosperous period.) Access to brickyards at Pembroke, Forester's Falls or Renfrew was a factor in the choice of building material, for unless the farm was on a good road, not too distant, or close to a railroad station, the transport of bricks to the site would be difficult.
The owner of this house was Ernest Schultz, father of seven children. He built it over a period of two years, 1909 to 1910, with the aid of several helpers including Herman Schultz (no relation) and Gustave Stresman.

Photograph reproduced courtesy Mrs. Mabel Stresman, Fraser Township.

GOOD LAND
In a fault valley on the Canadian Shield, which is well watered by tributaries of the Ottawa River, (the Muskrat, the Snake and the Bonnechere) most of the German farmers visited by William Sinn in October, 1860 had chosen their land, and later arrivals followed their example. Within this fault valley there are pockets of good soil that have not been eroded by glaciation, and in Alice and Wilberforce Townships fertile land could be found. On the Indian River in Alice Township, this land was selected by William Gorr in 1865; his farm is still owned and worked by his descendants, one of the German Century Farms in Renfrew County.

SMITHY IN A VILLAGE

Born in 1898, Bernhard Ristau (3rd gen.) was the last working general blacksmith in Renfrew County. His workshop at Golden Lake (seen in photo) was the place where anything from a frying pan to a child's sleigh was brought for repair. In addition to the usual forge and anvil, he had a wood-working lathe, on which he made handles for logging tools and farming tools. His smoky shed was the social centre for the men of the surrounding area.

SMITHY IN A TOWN
John Groehl, seen here in his workshop on Miller Street in 1952, was one of the last blacksmiths in Pembroke. He was one of the sons of Daniel Groehl of Green Lake, Wilberforce Township, an immigrant from Germany. Mr. Groehl had his training as a blacksmith at Thomas Pink's factory in Pembroke where logging tools were made.
Photograph by Carl Scheuneman, Petawawa

Also exhibiting at the Steam Engine Show, although his trade had never become outmoded in his lifetime was Henry Yeas, the last working blacksmith in the city of Pembroke; he worked at his two anvils at 620 McGee Street within a few days of his death in 1977, outlasting John Groehl and Bruno Eggert, also German blacksmiths in that community. Out in the countryside, the blacksmith's forge or the shed that contained a forge and associated equipment was a common feature on German farms. Not every farm had one, but the number of anvils and bellows that emerge at auction sales on old German farms shows that many of the immigrants from Germany were skilled enough to do their own shoeing of the draught animals that were so essential on the farm.

The report of the immigration agent, William Sinn, in October 1860, does not list horses at all, but it records that six out of 53 German farms had a team (i.e. a pair) of oxen. The owners were Carl Ruhs, Friedrich Schutt, Christian Wasmund, Martin Budarick and Wilhelm Luloff of Wilberforce Township and Carl Ringel of Alice Township. Oxen were placid in nature, which was one of their great advantages over horses; they were used in clearing the land, drawing the plough and pulling wagons. They were harnessed in pairs by a yoke which was a piece of hardwood shaped like a rounded letter M, and which fitted over the necks of the animals in front of their shoulders. The yoke was held in place by U-shaped pieces of wood (ash or willow) which enclosed the ox's neck. From the centre of the yoke an iron chain extended back to the load. The ox-yoke was one of the tools that immigrants made.

Unlike the German immigrants who moved from the United States to southern Ontario, those who came from Germany to eastern Ontario had crossed an ocean and had not been able to bring horses with them. Walter Reiche of Wilberforce Township believes that his great-grandfather who arrived in Wilberforce Township in 1863 was the first in his area to own a horse. During the third quarter of the 19th century horses gradually replaced oxen in eastern Ontario. The number of German immigrants who had served in cavalry regiments during their period of military service before immigration may explain why so many of them were skilled as blacksmiths. Even in the thoroughly English village of Rockingham, Brudenell Township, where John S.J. Watson reigned over a community that was almost feudal, the blacksmith listed on the 1871 census was German-speaking Carl Potter. In Sebastopol Township Julius Eduard Ziebarth, father of eleven children, did blacksmithing chores for his neighbours in return for farm produce, though he lived on a farm. There were many farmers, such as August Lipke of Germanicus, whose ability at the forge enabled him to peform work for others and supplement his income. Where the farmer who had a blacksmith's shed might consider it a sideline to his main activity of farming, the small building that held his anvil, forge and other tools was left to gather dust when the farm no longer was a viable means of supporting a family.

In villages, those whose workshop was a place of business, open to trade from all comers, presided over a social centre more egalitarian than the church; it was a place where farmers met and exchanged news while the blacksmith attended to their needs. Two of the last working blacksmiths in the rural townships were Arthur Karl Bernhard Genrick, 1896-1979, who worked in Raglan Township, and Arnold Bernhard Ristau, 1897-1981, who continued working in his smoky smithy at Golden Lake until 1979 when ill-health forced his retirement. Blacksmiths such as Barney Ristau constructed their workshop at a prominent location, in his case near a crossroads community. In addition to shoeing horses, which was of prime importance in the years before the automobile, the blacksmith could make repairs to wagons sleighs, logging tools, axes and any job that required the heating and hammering of metal. In the 20th century the horse-drawn farming equipment was gradually replaced by mechanized tools, but change was slow on the small farms that were typical of eastern Ontario. Here the use of horses as draught animals persisted until the 1930s for skidding logs, bush work and haying.

In his 1857 brochure of information for intending immigrants, Mr. French had stated, "Settlers are never prevented from making farms on the wild lands of the Crown wherever they find them best adapted to their wants, and all who may have gone to live on them

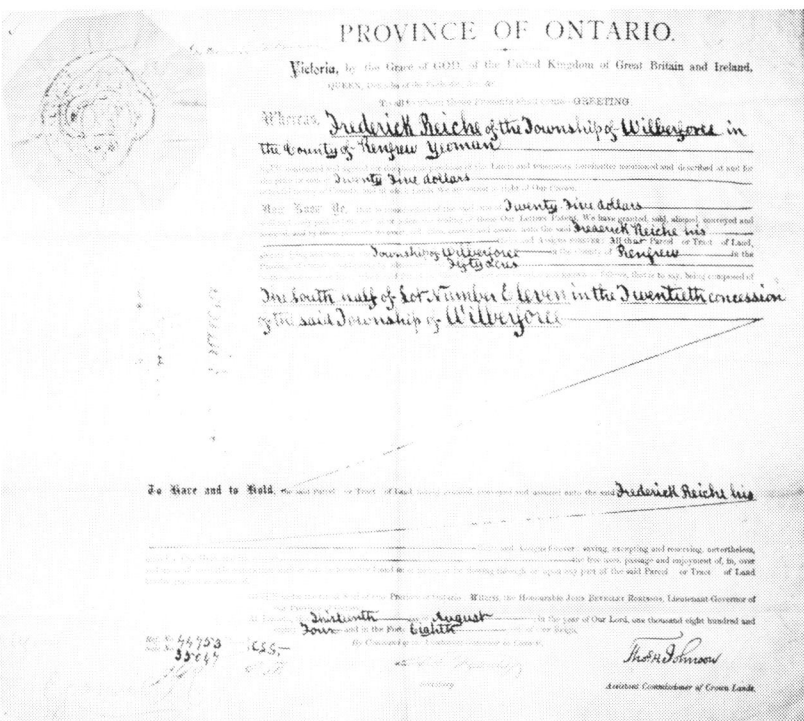

previous to their being sold, will be permitted a pre-emptive right to purchase". Mr. French could not have known that the offer of free grants of land on the colonization roads would be followed, in 1868, by another more widespread offer. "An Act respecting Free Grants and Homesteads to Actual Settlers on Public Lands" passed by the Legislative Assembly of the Province of Ontario, Feb. 28, 1868, conferred a legitimate title to any farmers who had simply squatted on land or those who were struggling to make payments on a piece of property that they were farming. Now it was theirs without fee. "The Free Grants and Homesteads Act" was only applicable to lands surveyed, or about to be surveyed, within the tract or territory composed of the Districts of Algoma and Nipissing, and of the lands lying between the Ottawa River and the Georgian Bay. The person to whom free land could be allotted had to be over the age of 18 years and could apply for as much as 200 acres. Some were content with half that amount.

Before any person was located for a free grant under this act of 1868, the applicant had to make an affidavit stating that he was the male head of a family, listing the number of dependents residing with him, and outlining the exact location of the land he wanted to possess. He had to make a declaration that the land for which he applied was suited for settlement and cultivation, and was not valuable chiefly for its mines, minerals, or pine timber; furthermore he had to make an assurance that the land was desired for his personal benefit, and for the purpose of actual settlement and cultivation. Specifically, he had to state that he did not expect to have any benefit or advantage from the discovery of gold, silver, copper, lead, iron or the quarrying of stone, marble or gypsum. This document had to be witnessed by someone who was well acquainted with the applicant and sworn before a commissioner who was appointed to accept such declarations.

The opportunity to own land was one of the major attractions of Eastern Ontario. The free grants offered by the Canadian government on the colonization roads, to immigrants from the British Isles and later to immigrants from Norway and Germany, were intended to open up a new agricultural region where Crown lands would be sold cheaply. Most of the German immigrants who came to Eastern Ontario elected to purchase land in the townships north of the Ottawa and Opeongo Road.
Frederick Reiche, 29, his wife Caroline and their one-year-old son, Erdman, emigrated from Austria (Oestreich) in 1863 and settled on lot 12, con. 19, Wilberforce Township, Renfrew County. The property was enlarged by purchase of neighbouring lots, such as this one in the document, lot 11, con. 20, which consisted of 50 acres purchased for the sum of $25 — or 50 cents an acre — in August 13, 1884.
This Century Farm, now owned by the 4th generation, Walter Reiche, now covers 450 acres, but its primary source of revenue is a slaughterhouse and a retail outlet for smoked meats.

who was well acquainted with the applicant and sworn before a commissioner who was appointed to accept such declarations.

When Robert August Hein applied for a Crown Grant of 200 acres under the 1868 act, on December 2, 1873, he asked to be located on lots 18, concession 11 and 12, in the Township of Lyndock. His affidavit was witnessed by Charles Tackman of the Township of Sebastopol, who affirmed that Hein was the male head of a family, consisting of three sons and two daughters under the age of 18 years of age. (There was no space on the document for any mention of a wife.) The commissioner in Sebastopol Township, F. Holterman, appears to have written most of the information on the document, but Robert Hein signed his own name, an ability that not every immigrant possessed.

By the time that Henry Raddatz was making his application for 200 acres in Sebastopol Township, June 27, 1887, the form that had to be filled out was becoming more complicated. Asking for lots four and five, concession eight in that township, he had to make a declaration about the condition of the land. In his case, he had to admit that some improvement had already been accomplished on the desired property; about 20 acres had been cleared by William Roy and 40 acres had been cleared by the applicant. A house that measured 20 feet by 20 feet had been constructed, also a barn that was 28 feet by 50 feet, a stable 20 feet by 30 feet and other buildings whose dimensions were not specified. Two acquaintances, Michael Milroy and Carl Rosin, both farmers in Sebastopol Township, now had to affirm that the applicant was telling the truth, and assure the commissioner, John Whelan, that Raddatz was the male head of a family having two sons. (The affidavit now had a provison for listing the sole female head of a family.) From the information contained on this document, it was obvious that some farmers were not bothering to make a formal application for their property until they had done considerable work on it. The date that appears on the actual document issued by the Province of Ontario to a Free Grant Settler may therefore be much later than the year that the settler located on that land. Census records that were conducted every ten years or township assessment rolls that were recorded annually may give another and earlier date.

No patent was issued for any land located under this act until five years had passed from the date of location, nor until the applicant had performed certain settlement duties. He was obliged to have cleared and have under cultivation at least 15 acres of the land, at the rate of at least two acres a year. A house fit for habitation, at least 16 feet by 20 feet, was a requirement and the applicant had to reside upon the property continuously during the term of five years succeeding the date of location, with the exception that he was allowed to be absent for a period that did not exceed six months in any one year provided that the land was cultivated. The latter provision allowed the farmer to take employment elsewhere during the winter months, and for most men this alternative source of income would be gained from a spell of work in a lumber camp. Some immigrants had a special skill that might be in demand in the towns.

The free grant of 100 acres awarded to William Gutzman, for lot no. 20 in the fifth concession of the township of Petawawa, on August 1, 1878, shows that he was located on that land under the provisions of "The Free Grants and Homesteads Act of 1868" on April 23, 1870. That was the first year that he appears on the assessment rolls of Petawawa Township as an occupant of land and a payer of taxes. It would be eight more years before he had fulfilled all the provisions of the Act and could claim his land without any payment. Actually, William Gutzman had immigrated before 1870, because he was already in the locality working as a tailor when the family of Gustave Michel arrived. The grandson of this immigrant, Oscar Michel, remembered that his grandparents had stayed with the tailor's family for the first winter, 1867-68, they spent in Petawawa Township.

In the 1871 census, William Gutzman, 39, and his wife, Carolin, 29, are listed as Lutherans from Pomerania, with three children, and his occupation was given as farmer. He had constructed a house and had improved the necessary two acres in his first year. His assets comprised five bushels of oats, 20 cords of firewood, one milk cow, two cattle, one live pig and one slaughtered pig and 50 pounds of butter. He must have felt contented with his progress, for other members of his family appear in the township assessment rolls in subsequent years. With spellings of the surname as Goodsman, the brother named Charles or Carl, aged 21, appears in 1871 and another brother named August aged 28, makes an appearance in 1873. It was the news of success of the first immigrants that encouraged more settlers to leave Germany, even after that country had been united and had become peaceful.

THE BLACKSMITH'S FAMILY LOOKED PROSPEROUS. c. 1895

John Lau came to Canada in 1891 with his wife, Alvina and two small daughters, Alma and Zelma. The family settled at Rankin in the township of Wilberforce where John Lau made his living as a blacksmith. The parents were photographed with their daughters and a son, Arthur, at a photographer's studio in Pembroke. There were several blacksmiths at Rankin in the late decades of the 19th century. Judging from this photograph the Laus must have done well. A second son, Verner, was born to this couple, but there are no persons of this surname in the Rankin area in 1986.

Photograph reproduced courtesy Locksley-Rankin Women's Institute.

When photographic studios opened in Pembroke and Renfrew in the last decade of the 19th century, portraits of satisfied settlers were sometimes taken for the express purpose of reassuring the family that they had left behind in Germany. Photographers seldom penetrated the rural townships, with the exception of one that used to make trips to Eganville, but those who lived in the country were visited by travelling artists who sketched their likenesses in black and white. Their handiwork has left an impression of first and second generation immigrants of German descent (as well as other ethnic groups) who look as if they are well-clothed and well-fed. The struggle to achieve self-sufficiency on small farms in a hostile environment does not show in their faces.

REASSURING THE FOLKS BACK HOME. c. 1900
Michael John Blimkie, with his wife and six children, emigrated from Germany to eastern Ontario in 1889. The couple had two more children after their arrival, Martin and Paul, and this photograph was taken at Neapole's Studio in Pembroke with their two Canadian-born sons, to send to relatives in Germany.

The Blimkies' move to Canada had been prompted by letters from others in their district (Pomerania) who had emigrated in earlier years and had been pleased with their new country. Michael, who was 48 when he emigrated, had been a farmer in Germany and he had sold his farm in order to bring his family to Canada. He bought a house in Pembroke but it took him about a year to obtain a full-time job; he worked for the town and this helped him to learn English. His wife, Mary Anna Hanneman Blimkie, never really mastered the language of her new surroundings and by the time that her grandchildren were growing up they would speak to her in English but she would reply in German.

THE SECOND GENERATION
In the 1890s an artist travelled around the farms of Renfrew County, sketching portraits and occasionally full-length studies, such as this one of Arnold Ristau, the father of Bernhard Ristau, the blacksmith at Golden Lake until 1979.

The parents of Arnold Ristau had eight young children, six sons and two daughters, when they emigrated from Pinne, Posen, in the early 1880s. They settled on a farm in South Algona Township.

Arnold Ristau married Emilia Schultz and began a family in 1893. This sketch was probably made in his bachelor days, for it was customary for husbands and wives to be sketched together. The second generation of the German people in eastern Ontario looked content and even prosperous; at any rate they could afford an occasional luxury, such as sitting for an artist.

THE SECOND GENERATION BY 1909

Mr. and Mrs. William Schroeder (second and third from right) were photographed outside their home in Petawawa Township one day when relatives were visiting. The sons and daughters of German immigrants had by that time acquired a substantial log farmhouse and enjoyed a degree of self-sufficiency on small farms. This building, with its logs covered by siding, is occupied by a daughter of Mr. and Mrs. William Schroeder.

Photograph reproduced courtesy Mrs. Freda McNab, Petawawa Twp.

EARNING MONEY AT THE LUMBER CAMPS
In the bunkhouse of a logging camp in Northern Ontario, circa 1917, a group of German farmers' sons from Petawawa Township are relaxing; some are members of the Gust or Weissenberg families.

Photo courtesy of Adolph Gust, Petawawa.

In the dining room of Camp #4 at Massey, Northern Ontario, 1912-1913. The 16-year-old cook on the right was Charles Bochart of Eganville, who loaned this photograph. Winter work at the lumber camps was a tradition for three generations of farmers in Renfrew County.

THE SECOND GENERATION

The daughter of German immigrants who arrived in North Algona in 1867, Anna Wilhelmina Louisa Luloff was married April 3, 1981, to a cousin, John Luloff, a son of German immigrants who had settled in Grattan Township. Widowed in 1909, this mother of four children remained in charge of her 340-acre farm near Augsburg until her late 90s, dying at the age of 100 years and six months.

Mingled with the Irish settlers and bordered by Polish neighbours the German-Canadians of the 19th century married people who could also speak German, the language used in their churches and their homes. Almost all German immigrants belonged to Protestant faiths — Lutherans, Baptists, Methodists and Evangelicals — and this was another obstacle to intermarriage with their neighbours who were members of the Roman Catholic Church. It was not uncommon for a widow to marry her brother-in-law, or for a widower to marry his sister-in-law, and cousins married occasionally.

In the generation who grew up in the early years of the 20th century, there was very little choice of marriage partner for those who lived in the western townships of the county where there were no roads until 1934. As a result, some of the long-established family farms there are now in the possession of elderly people who have no direct descendants because they have never married.

The 1971 census showed a decline in the number of people of German origin in Renfrew County, 12,865 down from 14,014 in 1961. This was the first decline in more than a century of censuses.

MUD-LAKE ANNIE
The only daughter of Mr. and Mrs. Johann Luloff, born one year after they left Germany and came to Golden Lake in 1867, Annie Luloff retained her surname when she married her cousin, John. She had two sisters-in-law called Annie, which caused confusion, so Mrs. Ferdinand Luloff became known as Ferny's Annie and Mrs. Edward Luloff was known as Eddie's Annie. Mrs. John Luloff, who was widowed in 1909, lived on a farm in Grattan Township, beside a widening of the Bonnechere River known as Mud Lake and this gave her the unflattering nickname of Mud-Lake Annie. She is remembered in the Augsburg area as a shrewd woman who ran her 340-acre farm competently until her ninth decade. She danced on her 92nd birthday when this photograph was taken by the local Lutheran pastor. She was still spinning at the age of 95 years. Following her death, Nov. 19, 1968, at the age of 100 years, six months, the obituary in The Eganville Leader commented: "She was a quiet woman whose only pleasure was in the creation of her own hands, helping a neighbour in time of need and actively supporting her church." She had outlived her husband, four brothers and three of her four children.

Photograph reproduced courtesy Mrs. August (Joyce) Miller, Augsburg.

GERMAN CRAFTSMANSHIP?
Richard White, who was Mayor of Pembroke, 1862-1864, bought 150 acres one mile east of the town, c. 1865, and "put men at work clearing it". This was a decade in which immigrants from Germany were earning money in Pembroke in order to purchase land. The carpenters who built Richard White's house may have been German, for the apical ornaments on the gables of this farmhouse are similar to those found in Pommern (Pomerania), according to illustrated books on the subject.

Photographed in 1974, the unoccupied house is deteriorating.

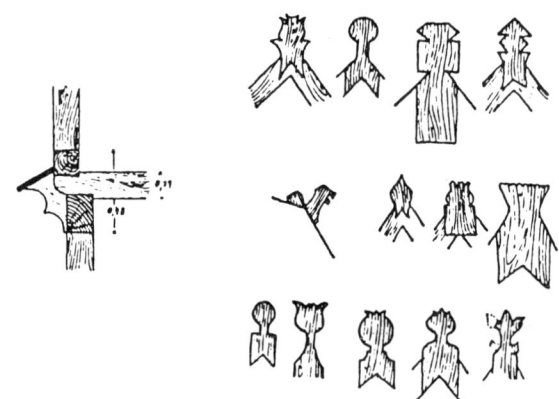

Examples of apical ornaments are gables on farmhouses built in the Pyritz area of Pommern, which were illustrated in "Das Baurnhaus Im Deutschen Reiche" by Dr. Dietrich Schafer. He wrote: "Gable ornaments can be found on almost every house, often on front and back."

Chapter III.

Keeping Warm and fed

Throughout the colonial history of Canada the great majority of settlers came from the agricultural classes of their home lands: French peasants, American farmers, English labourers, Scottish crofters and Irish potato farmers. Few of them had actually owned land, although some of them had been tenant farmers. Historians have concluded that it was the lure of land ownership that drew so many of these immigrants, though their backgrounds were varied. Some were inadequately prepared to tackle the wilderness. Scottish crofters exiled from their highlands and Irish tenants forced from their homes by a potato famine came from a background that was limited in its agricultural practices.

By contrast, the immigrants from a countryside that is now part of northern and eastern Germany came from a fertile and well-watered land where a great variety of crops and livestock flourished. The principal products included wheat, corn, timber, hemp, flax, oats, barley, peas, rye, potatoes, provisons and ashes. Little land was rented and the cultivation of large estates was performed by labourers who had few luxuries. The wages of a farm labourer varied from summer to winter; his wooden or clay cottage was either free or provided at a low rental and he had a garden and pasture for a cow. Potatoes, rye bread and milk were the common ingredients of his family's diet. Though he might work for landlords in the cultivation of the above-named crops, he was unlikely to attain independence as a landowner. Little wonder then that those who arrived in eastern Ontario were content to buy less than 100 acres of land initially; a parcel of 50 acres was considered a sizeable farm, according to many descendants who can recall their grandparents' tales.

While all those who settled on the Canadian Shield had to contend with the problems of the clearing of the land and fencing it before grazing livestock and crops could become part of their livelihood, there was one source of revenue that could be tapped immediately — if the farm had a grove of maple trees. In his book of information for intending immigrants, the Crown Lands Agent, T.P. French had alluded to this natural food, which would be unknown to any settlers that came from Britain or continental Europe. He wrote, "Imported sugar is seldom seen by settlers in the bush, but that which they make themselves from the sap of the maple tree answers all their purposes quite as well. The process of sugar-making is extremely simple, and being unattended by any expense, all settlers make a little, while some make and sell a great deal annually".

It was true enough that the maple syrup could be produced from a raw material to a finished product without much expense, but it was false to assume that every farm had a stand of maple trees, and only the sugar maple (Acer saccarum) has sap in sufficient quantity and sugar content. Preparation of sugar from the maple's watery sap was discovered by the Indians, who passed on the technique to the colonists in North America. In eastern Ontario the German immigrants most probably learned this skill from the British farmers who preceded them.

The quantity of maple syrup produced in any season is dependent on the weather. In the spring of 1980 and 1981 the March weather was exceptionally mild, and sugar bushes on low ground could not be worked. According to Mrs. Eleanor Tiegs, Grattan Township, "The sap stays in the trees if the nights are not cold enough". Mrs. Tiegs' sugar bush was on low ground. On the hills above the Ottawa and Opeongo Colonization Road in Sebastopol Township, the more exposed maple trees were being tapped on two farms that had large numbers of trees and an operation that might be termed semi-commercial in nature. On many farms in eastern Ontario, the spring ritual of tapping the maples is an event that produces just enough syrup for the immediate family. The run of sap lasts less than a month, buckets are used to collect it and the boiling down (to concentrate it) may be done in the kitchen, much to the dismay of the housewife who has to clean up the remains of the sticky vapours.

On the farms of the Kosmacks and the Drefkes, which had both been enlarged from the original colonization road grant of 100 acres, the extent of the maple bush made it necessary to construct a sugar shanty; the location of this shanty reduced the toil involved in transporting the sap from the trees to the place where most of the boiling down occurred. The sap requires a reduction in volume, as much as 40-fold, before it has the thick consistency of syrup.

STUMP-PULLER
The agent in Germany who was recruiting settlers for eastern Ontario, 1860-1862, suggested that the most suitable immigrants would be "a people used to tearing out the stumps of trees from the soil." George Bartscher of Grattan Township shows how a stumping-jack was used (for demonstration purposes the jack was suspended from a barn door lintel). Leverage on the long handle pumped the notched spine up in jerks and pulled the stump out of the ground. These iron tools were made by blacksmiths and Mr. Bartscher believed that this stumping-jack was made by Ernst Bimm of Eganville. When the Bartschers moved from South Algona Township in 1916 to an Irish farm in a more fertile part of Renfrew County, the young men in the family, such as George and his brothers, completed the clearance of stumps from the fields; they used a stump-puller and a stumping-jack.

STONES AND TIMBER MAKE A FENCE
Clearing the land of obstacles, such as trees, then stumps, and finally stones, provided the settlers on the Canadian Shield with plenty of material to enclose their lands. Fences were needed to keep the livestock from wandering, and from encroaching on fields where crops were growing. In this scene of a stone-and-timber fence in South Algona Township, it would appear that there were plenty of stones left in the field, even though this land has been worked for over a century.

SELLING THE STONES
It was possible for some settlers to make money from the stones that littered their land. A group of German farmers from Sebastopol Township are unloading a wagonload of stones that they have hauled to Eganville. (The farmer, at extreme right, is Frederick Kosmack, son of Albert Kosmack, an immigrant.)

Men and teams were employed by the municipality of Eganville to transport stones to this village, so that they could be crushed and laid upon the muddy streets. In 1903 a stone crusher was purchased from the Sawyer-Massey Co. of Hamilton. A special meeting of the village council authorized the reeve to sign an agreement with Mr. J.D. McRae, to supply electric power to operate the crusher for one month in each year. The agreement was made for five years and Mr. McRae (who owned the power plant on the Bonnechere River which runs through Eganville) was to receive $110 every month he furnished power, according to a report in The Eganville Leader, June 24, 1903.

Photograph reproduced courtesy Allan Kosmack, Sebastopol Township.

On the farm of Verner Drefke the shanty was a crude structure which sheltered both the pans of boiling sap and the workers from the elements; nearby trees had the traditional spouts or 'spiles' driven into the trunks, through which the sap dripped into buckets, but plastic tubing drained the sap from many trees on sloping ground and conveyed to it by gravity into large containers.

On the farm of Allan Kosmack and his sons, Glenn and Morley, the trees were being tapped individually into buckets, but a tractor-driven wagon, loaded with barrels, was being driven around the property in order to collect the large volume of sap and transport it to the modern shanty. There the watery liquid was boiled down and a thermometer used to assess when the critical temperature had been reached. The quantity of syrup produced on farms where hundreds of maple trees can be sapped provides a source of revenue at a time when most farming activities are dormant.

One activity that engaged the men during the winter season, if they had not gone to the lumber camps, was the production of tools that would help them and their wives live off the land.

Neck-yokes were made for the carrying of water from the well. Other yokes were needed to harness oxen. For cereal crops the chaff forks, rakes and grain shovels were all necessary. Sauerkraut cutters were made to help shred cabbage. Equipment for the manufacture of textiles ranged from the large and bulky loom to the niddy-noddy that was used to wind yarn. There were some tools, such as the spinning-wheels, that only the most skilled immigrants could make from the local woods, and there were some tools, such as the reaper and the scythe, that would have to be purchased.

From the report of the 1860 harvest prepared by the immigration agent, William Sinn, who visited the German farms in Renfrew County that fall, it is apparent that wheat and potatoes were the crops produced in most abundance; oats were third in quantity, followed by peas and barley. He noted that the settlers had trouble transporting their crops to the grist mills in Pembroke and Eganville, because there were no regular roads in Alice and Wilberforce Townships. Water-powered grist mills which served the residents of the townships along the Ottawa River had been established in this county in 1858. There were two at Renfrew, owned by John McRae and John Lorne McDougall, and the facilities at this village were accessible to all those who had located along the Ottawa and Opeongo Colonization Road; other grist mills already in existence were John Egan's at Eganville, Alexander Moffatt's at Pembroke, James Condie's at Beachburg, Nathaniel Burwash's at Arnprior and Charles Merrick's at Douglas. Of these, only the ones at Eganville and Pembroke were within easy travelling distance for the German farmers who had settled in greatest numbers in the townships of North and South Algona, Wilberforce, Alice, Petawawa and Stafford.

John Watson's grist mill in Brudenell Township was built on Rockingham Creek in 1860, followed by one at Killaloe, Hagarty Township, on Brennan Creek in 1871; the village of Denbigh in Lennox and Addington County (just over the border of Renfrew County) had its own grist mill by 1868 built by Charles and Paul Stein, a father and son from Germany. However, the later mills were located on smaller and placid waterways; the earlier mills had been built on larger rivers which had a more powerful current and precipitous falls. Threshing and milling were exclusively winter jobs at that time, because the frost-hardened ground enabled the farmer to team heavy sleighloads, assuming he had horses to tackle the task. Stories of how some settlers had to carry 100 pound bags of grain on their backs to a mill are legion and even the wives of some German farmers are known to have undertaken this arduous errand.

The first cultivation of crops might begin before the land had been totally cleared of obstacles such as stumps and boulders. Mr. French advised that the grain could be sown by hand and simply dragged or harrowed in without any previous plowing. Harvesting the grain was also done by hand, the reaper being replaced by the scythe, and the scythe by the cradle. The reaper and the scythe were both on the list of tools considered essential to the newly arrived immigrant. While the reaping sickle required the operator to bend as he cut the stalks one-handed close to the ground, the scythe allowed a standing man to sweep the blade along the ground while he swung it sideways with both arms. The cradle was essentially a scythe with an added wooden frame above the three-foot blade. On this the cut grain fell, the straws lying neatly parallel, so that the crop was collected in bundles as it was reaped and deposited on the ground. It required a man with stamina to use a cradle because of the added weight of the cut grain on the wooden frame; the tying of bundles of grain could be done by the less hearty members of the family who followed behind and who set them upright in the field in 'stooks' to dry, before taking them to the barn for threshing and storage. On some of the fields that have been cultivated by German farmers for over a century, the stones keep coming to the surface with every ploughing and as long as the farmer grew cereal crops the use of the grain cradle was not outmoded, for mechanized or even horse-drawn equipment could not be used.

Hand-threshing with a flail was commonly performed by the immigrants, of all nationalities, in eastern Ontario in the 19th century, and some descendants can remember it. The flail was simply a club, swivelled with leather at the end of a handle about six feet long, and this was another farming tool that the farmer could make himself. Inside the barn, threshing was performed by thumping the cereal crop with this club until the kernels were knocked out of the heads onto the barn floor. After it had been thoroughly threshed, the straw was gathered up, with the aid of a home-made fork, and stored for use as animal bedding. On some German farms a special

device known as a straw-cutter (streuschneider) was made, either with a hardwood blade honed to a fine edge or with an iron blade obtained from the local blacksmith; this was a wooden trough into which the straw was clamped so that the blade would chop through the stalks. A wooden shovel, often carved from basswood, the lightest of Canadian hardwoods, was made by some farmers to gather up the grain.

GRAIN SHOVEL
The reverse side of this grain shovel, made by Carl Gutzman (1850-1936), shows the fine carving skill of this German furniture-maker, who made it for use on his farm in Petawawa Township. At an auction sale in 1981, this shovel sold for $100.

MAKING MAPLE SYRUP
Verner Drefke, 65, third generation from immigrant Carl Drefke from Germany, was tapping 900 maple trees and making 20 gallons of syrup a day in the spring of 1980. His sugar shanty, on steep ground covered with boulders, had evaporating pans inside and out, with chimneys to carry away the wood-smoke. The Drefke property, on the Opeongo Road in Sebastopol Township, had expanded to 400 acres from the original Crown Grant of 100 acres. "Information for intending settlers on the Ottawa and Opeongo Road", published 1857, included this passage: "The manufacture of Maple-Sugar may take place before farming operations commence in the Spring, with advantage to the settler and without involving the loss of any valuable labor". Not all the farms had maple trees.

TOOLS MADE FROM BASSWOOD
Basswood is one of the softest and lightest in weight of the Canadian hardwoods. The pioneering settlers found it to be useful for hand-carved tools such as the grain shovel. The basswood's lack of taste or odour also made it valuable for food containers, such as this rectangular bowl which was used for mixing ground meat. Both these tools were made by Julius Albert Zadow, who emigrated from Steinburg-in-Neumark in 1881, at the age of 27, bringing with him a large pine chest which contained woodworking tools. One descendant has the curved hand adze which was used to carve these pieces from basswood.

NECK-YOKE

Neck-yokes, carved from a solid piece of wood, made it easier to carry a couple of buckets of water from the well to the house. The load was balanced evenly on the shoulders. William Walther of Vanbrugh, Sebastopol Township, was using this neck-yoke to aid the task of moving potatoes from his vegetable garden to his root cellar. The yoke was made by Robert Redtman of Arnprior.

RECTANGULAR BOWL
Keith Schleuter holding a large rectangular bowl made by his great-grandfather Matthew Horcun, in Hagarty Township. Mr. Schleuter is a farmer who keeps cattle and works the land of his ancestors still. The smokehouse and the wooden bowl for mixing ground meat for the sausages are no longer needed by the fourth generation, but the reminders of a self-sufficient past are not discarded.

CHAFF FORK
This chaff fork, made from local hardwoods, could have been used by the same German immigrant who squared the timbers to build the barn that held the cereal crops and hay that were harvested on this farm in South Algona Township.

THRESHING WITH HORSE POWER
In Hagarty Township where the pioneer farmers were immigrants from Germany, Ireland and Poland, threshing was one of the communal efforts where neighbours of different origins and languages worked together. In this photograph, taken on the farm of John Holly, some of the men have been identified as William Lisk, Antoine Borutskie, Matthew Noack II, Herman Wolfgram, John Blaedow, Matthew Okum, John Holly, August Noack, Albert Noack and William Noack. Teams of horses are treading a circular path, attached to long poles that rotate a central device that provides power.

Photograph reproduced courtesy Matthew Noack III, Hagarty Township.

THE SIZE OF THE LOGS

On the Behm century farm, concession one, Bromley Township, there were massive timbers available for the German immigrant, August Behm, (1860-1910) who built his first home here before Confederation. That house was replaced by the second owner, Fred Behm (who married Pauline Bramberger) with a substantial brick dwelling, but when the timbers were dismantled by a grandson, Henry Behm, and his son Irwin, some of the squared logs were used to construct a pighouse. August Behm's grandson believes that the immigrant left Germany after completing his mandatory three years of military service and came to Renfrew County with a brother named Herman. He was a member of the Lutheran church at Northcote, now vanished, but is buried at Eganville, near the grave of his second wife.

Threshing by horse power was one of those farming activities that saw neighbours combining their efforts and their horses. One type of horse treadmill was designed like an oversized capstan, with horses hitched to the ends of four arms that were attached to a central machine. Whereas a one-horse model could be used by one farmer within his own farm, the multiple-horse circle needed more space for the animals to tramp around in a circle, causing a central shaft to turn and transmit motion. It was a communal effort, requiring several teams and several men.

The first steam-powered threshing machine to be used in Renfrew County was displayed in 1882 by Xavier Plaunt at his farm near Renfrew. The capital cost of a stationary steam engine, one that could power tasks such as threshing on the farm, was too high for an individual to acquire solely for his own use on a few hundred acres, and most of the farms in eastern Ontario were still quite small. There were farmers like Bernhard Schutt of Germanicus, who had invested in a steam-threshing outfit in 1906, replacing the horse-powered thresher which he had used in the 1890s. This portable steam engine, on wheels, was hauled by horses from farm to farm in Wilberforce Township in the fall, to thresh a farmers' crops within his granary. Wood fuelled the engine, water filled the boilers and two men could tackle the farm-grain harvest in one day or less, even if they had to work late in the light of oil-lamps.

In 1912, Mr. Schutt threshed for 71 German farmers, in 1913 for 88 farmers and in 1914 for 81 German farmers starting on the first day of September (see table in this chapter). While all his customers have German names, by now most of these farms were in the hands of farmers' sons, born in Wilberforce Township. When the threshing season had ended, sometime in November, Mr. Schutt's steam engine was used to grind mixed grain into feed for livestock. For this job the steam-powered grinder was set up in a field, near a well, and customers brought their produce to the site.

Record of steam-threshing for other farmers, in 1914, by B. Schutt, in Wilberforce Township, beginning September 1.

P. Brose. 7.00
H. Lubo. 5.00
C. Schutt. 6.75
H. Wolfgram. 4.00
W. Wolfgram. 5.50
Frank Sack. 7.00
A. Sperberg. 4.00
A. Luloff. 5.50
F. Sack. 6.50
W. Hine. 5.00
H. Hahs. 7.00
R. Gahr. 6.00
F. Schultz. 5.00
G. Reckzin. 6.00
D. Kohlmaier. 6.00
H. Hunt. 6.00
R. Schultz. 5.00
F. Komm. 6.50
A. Miller. 12.50
J. Leman 5.50
A. Laman 4.50
G. Junop 5.50
F. Kohl. 8.50
W. Bernt. 8.50
G. Krantz. 6.75
E. Luloff. 8.50
C. Hildebrandt. 4.25
B. Quast. 5.50
E. Rusler. 4.50
H. Schimmen. 5.50
J. Ruslir. 4.50
H. Bredlau. 3.00
P. Psaow. 8.50
J. Bohn. 10.50
J. Blodow. 8.00
F. Tur. 6.50
W. Springer. 9.00
W. Batz. 4.00
H. Witzel. 8.00
W. Fridrick. 11.00
Jo. Sell. 3.50
J. Butt. 4.00
W. Hildebrandt. 5.00
E. Rickzen. 4.00
A. Lipke. 6.50
H. Luloff. 6.00
J. Hain. 6.00
A. Hain. 5.50
H. Kutchke. 8.00
H. Krone. 5.00
H. Wolfgram 4.50
J. Stashnick. 2.50
E. Schunaman. 8.00
J. Biederman. 5.00
E. Brose. 8.50
A. Biderman. 12.50
H. Rieglen. 10.00
J. Schultz. 2.50
Frank Wolfgram. 6.50
W. Karow. 4.00
W. Moritz. 4.00
G Felske. 4.00
C. Siegle. 6.50
J. Schroder. 7.00
F. Schiscoske. 6.50
J. Nauman. 6.50
S. Woller. 5.00
C. Kopke. 6.00
C. Raglin. 6.00
T. Radtke. 4.00
H. Griefe. 5.00
F. Yante. 5.50
C. Grief. 6.00
F. Sill. 5.50
E. Reicher. 5.00
D. Grohl. 6.00
O. Sill. 4.50
H. Sill. 4.50
W. Wienhols. 6.75

Total calculated as $468.55.

Proceeds from the 1916 threshing season totalled $501.75, but repairs to the John Goodison threshing mill cost $401, and were paid in cash.

Record of grain-grinding (crushing grain) for other farmers, in 1914, in Wilberforce Township, on November 20, by B. Schutt.

W. Hine. 680 lbs 40c
H. Schonfelt. 1185 lbs. 70c
A. Hine. 1035 lbs. 62c
P. Brose. 1000 lbs. 60c
H. Luloff. 1310 lbs. 80c
P. Brose. 965 lbs. 58c
P. Brose. 1080 lbs. 62c
W. Reckzine. 630 lbs. 38c
H. Wolfgram. 745 lbs. 45c
W. Sack. 525 lbs. 30c
A. Kant. 675 lbs. 40c
H. Luloff. 1000 lbs. 60c
H. Schonfelt. 1035 lbs. 63c
W. Schonfelt. 1000 lbs. 60c
P. Brose. 4695 lbs. $3.80
H. Kutzschke. 1435 lbs. 85c
Gahr. 500 lbs. 30c
G. Reckzin. 525 lbs. 31c
R. Gahr. 625 lbs. 34c
F. Schultz. 400 lbs. 25c

Total calculated as $9.86.

Records reproduced courtesy K.G. Schutt, Killaloe.

Son, Gerhard Schutt of Killaloe, explains that a portable steam engine would be set up at a well in a field, with a long belt extended to a grinder where grain was crushed. Farmers would bring big wagon- or sleigh-loads of mixed grain to be crushed into provender. This grain-grinding operation was only done for a few days each year.

(The spellings of surnames may not be the same, but some descendants may recognise the names of their families. B.L-W.)

Records reproduced courtesy K.G. Schutt, Killaloe.

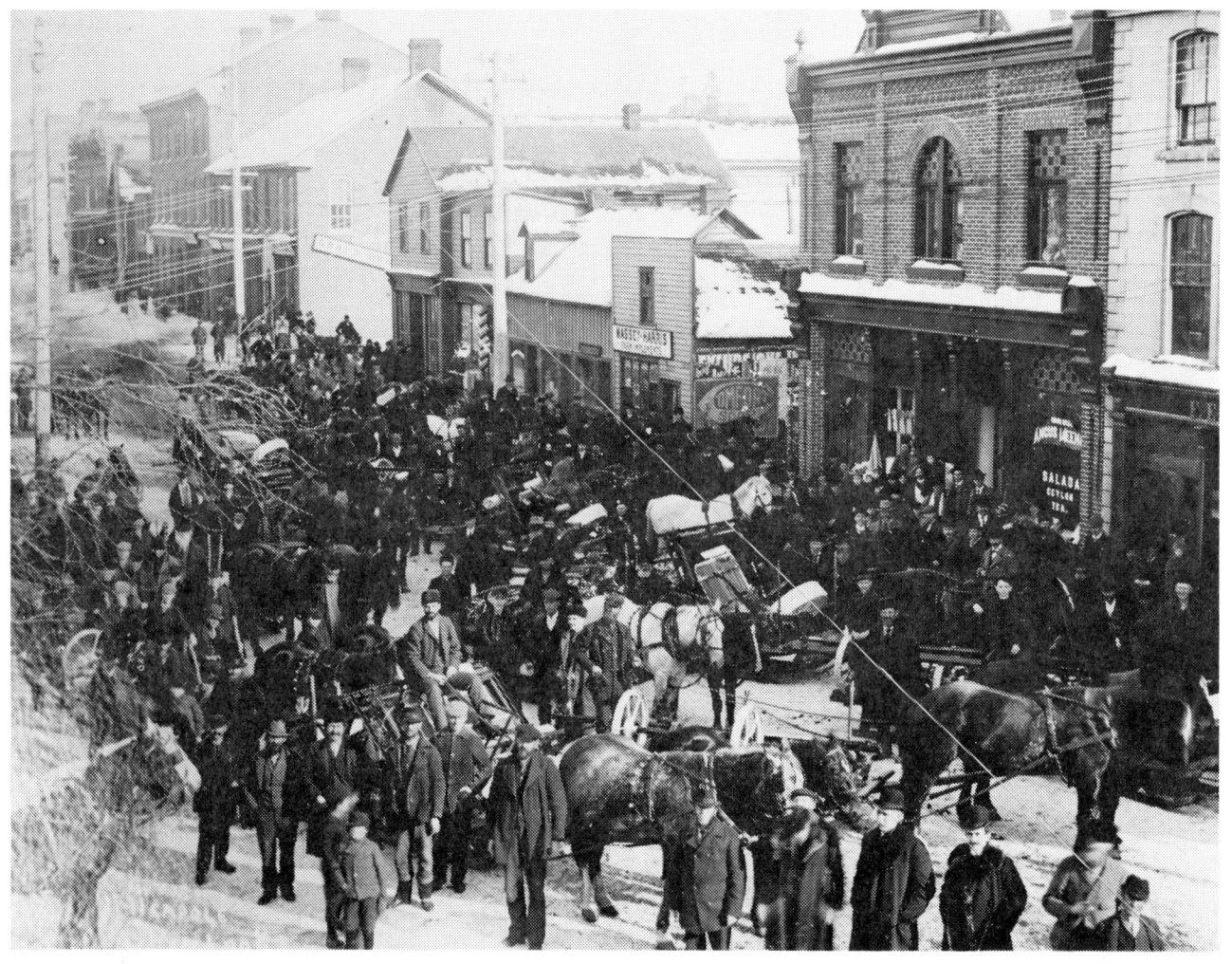

DELIVERY DAY. c. 1905.
Pembroke and Eganville were two centres where farmers collected the farm machinery they had ordered from agents of the manufacturer. The equipment arrived by rail on a selected day in late winter, when the roads were still hard enough for farmers to take home heavy machinery drawn by teams of horses. The Massey-Harris agent in Pembroke (small store in the centre with false front) appears to have had a successful sale of his company's products.

Photograph reproduced courtesy Champlain Trail Museum, Pembroke.

In 1913 the Pembroke Mill erected one of the largest grain elevators in eastern Canada, one which had a capacity of 15,000 bushels. Bulk-handling had already become a common practice on the prairies, where a new large area was more suitable by soil and climate for the production of wheat. Although the first world war provided an impetus to wheat-growing on small farms and the grist mills that served them, the farmers in Renfrew County had another market closer at hand for the crops that grew here.

The winter camps of the logging companies were moving farther and farther up the Ottawa Valley with every passing year. A winter road which had been built parallel to the Ottawa River, allegedly as a colonization road from Pembroke to Mattawa, was a convenient route for the farmers of Renfrew County to take their own crops and produce directly to the consumer. Along the Pembroke and Mattawan Road, at intervals, there were stopping-places where the teamster and his horse-drawn sleigh could pause for the night. The higher prices obtained at lumber camps more than compensated for the cost of the trip. Mrs. Rose Yeas of Pembroke can remember her father, Albert Carl Brasch, setting out in a cavalcade of eight to ten sleighs from Alice Township. They would then leave their farms on a Monday and be back by the end of the week. Mr. Brasch used to take loads of potatoes, which would freeze during their journey on the sleigh; he told his daughter that the lumber camp cooks would keep them frozen in piles out of doors and throw them into the pot when needed.

In 1905 a load of 80 bushels of oats would yield $56 when sold directly by the farmer who teamed it himself to the lumber camp, whereas the same quantity on the home market would yield only $27.50. The expenses of this journey for the farmer, who had taken with him feed for his horses and himself, would amount to $6 for the entire trip, including pay to a man to do chores at home. A profit of $12.80 was realized. As late as 1917 farmers in the Eganville area, such as Charles Bochert, still found it profitable to drive sleigh-loads of crops to the lumber shanties. Mr. Bochert could remember spending one night at a stopping-place at Deep River run by the King family.

When the immigration agent, William Sinn, visited German families in Renfrew County in 1860, he found that virtually every household had one or two dairy cows which were needed to provide milk and dairy products for the household. At first the farmer's wife made butter from the surplus milk solely for her own family's needs. When production began to exceed home requirements the extra butter was exchanged for cash or merchandise at the local general stores in Killaloe, Eganville, Golden Lake, Renfrew and Pembroke. Advertisements from merchants in the local weekly newspapers offered to buy butter by the tub or by the pound or take it in exchange. The volume traded in to merchants became so great that it attracted buyers who collected it for transport to the cities or for export to countries abroad. As early as September 1872, the following advertisement appeared in The Renfrew Mercury:

"Butter! Butter! 600 package wanted by the first of November, as the Subscriber has made arrangements to ship to England in November, by the last Steamer in Montreal, 55,000 lbs of Choice Butter. He will pay a higher price than anyone else for the above quantity of A-1 butter. W. Ferguson. Butter to be delivered at R. Airth's (The People's Tea Store) or at W. and J. Tierney's Dry Goods and Clothing Store. W.F." The total export of butter from Canada that year was 19,068,448 lbs, which travelled to Great Britain and the United States.

The quality of butter traded in by the farmer's wife would vary, depending on her skill and her equipment. Shallow trays were used at first for the separation of the cream and churns were employed to mix and pound the cream until the butter was formed. The dash churn, an upright wooden or stoneware vessel, had a lid that was pierced by a hole to permit the up-and-down operation of a long-handled cross-piece or 'dasher'. The barrel churn (or daisy churn) because it was larger and easier to operate with its rotary dasher and foot-pedal, became popular in the early years of the 20th century. Eaton's catalogue of 1902 advertised it in three sizes; nine gallons at $3.85; 15 gallons at $4.15 and 20 gallons at $4.75. A churn was never filled more than half full — about 8 gallons in a 15 gallon churn — so that there was plenty of room for agitation. These churns were fitted with a tiny glass window at one end, so that the operator could determine when the butter had formed. The buttermilk could be drawn off by means of a bung-hole, and the butter was then well washed with cold water (in the churn) before being salted.

The operation of the barrel churn did not require so much skill and the children of the family were often conscripted for the task of making butter. Mrs. Wesley Budd continued to make butter on the farm in the traditional way until the day that she and her husband retired from the property one fall day in 1983; she even milked the

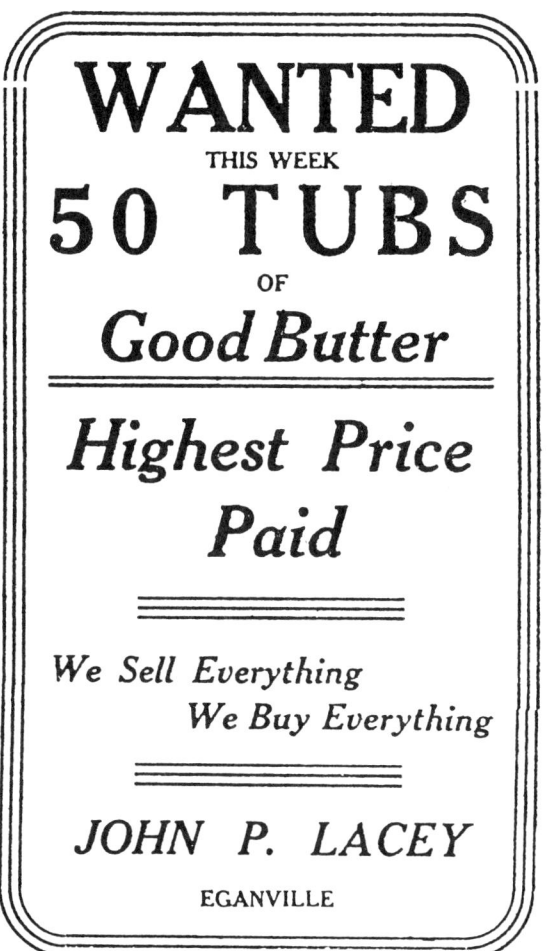

BUTTER WANTED
There were several merchants in Eganville who purchased farm produce such as butter and forwarded it to the cities for re-sale or export. Eganville was served by two railways and the Canada Atlantic Railway began to use chilled railway cars for the transport of butter in 1904.
The Eganville Leader. Sept. 8, 1911.

cows on the day of the auction sale. On the Budds' farm in Wilberforce Township there was a milk-shed, a wooden building set aside for the purpose of making dairy products. On some German farms the construction of a stone milkhouse was undertaken; it provided more insulation for the storage of milk, cream and butter during the months of warm weather. Building a structure from the local fieldstone must have required much more care and labour, but it must have been judged worthwhile during the years that the dairy industry provided a steady source of income for small farms.

Although almost every German household that Mr. Sinn visited in 1860 had a cow, the possession of swine was a close second in importance and a great deal higher in actual numbers. Making his records in October as he did, Mr. Sinn probably saw the porkers at their fittest and fattest, for the slaughter of pigs is commonly done in the last weeks of fall, just before wintry temperatures make outdoor chores unpleasant.

The Eganville Leader. Oct. 25, 1912.

Butter Wanted

We will Pay until Further Notice
Trade   28c.   per lb.
Cash   26c.   " "

We are selling Amercian Coal Oil at **12c** Per Gallon until December 31st, 1912.

JACOB KIZELL - Killaloe Station

KILLALOE STATION WAS ONCE A SHIPPING POINT

Construction of track for the Ottawa, Arnprior and Parry Sound Railway passed close to Killaloe in 1894, en route to its final terminus on Georgian Bay which it reached in 1897. Because it became the shipping centre for wool, livestock and dairy products from the surrounding countryside, Killaloe Station grew in importance as a community and the merchants there advertised for farmers' produce. In June 1904 the Department of Agriculture persuaded the Canada Atlantic Railway to begin running chilled railway cars in summertime for the transport of butter to Montreal. One of these special cars left Barry's Bay every Wednesday; Killaloe Station was the third stop on its route.

The Eganville Leader. Oct. 25, 1912.

MAKING BUTTER

On a German farm in Wilberforce Township, this housewife was making butter, just for her own family, using a barrel churn that had been connected to an electric motor to make the work easier. The white pail holds the buttermilk and the brown crock contains the butter which she was scooping out of the churn. On this farm, which was established by William Fick from Germany, c. 1872, the third and fourth generation still had a small dairy herd and were selling the milk to a Pembroke dairy. In pioneering years each farm would have at least one cow for the supply of dairy products for the individual family.

WOODEN BUTTER CHURN AND DASHER

The wooden dasher churns, shaped like a conical keg and tapered at the top, were generally made by coopers. The staves of cedar or oak were steamed and fitted together, then held in place by metal hoops, ensuring a container that did not leak. The base of the lids were made of wood and the dasher was a long wooden handle that slid through a hole in the top. At the end of the handle was a cross or circular plunger which agitated the cream, when pressed up and down repeatedly in the churn, until the butter had separated from the buttermilk. This churn was used on a farm that was first occupied by a German family in 1867 and maintained by three generations over a period of 115 years. Later churns of this type were made of pottery or stoneware and both were supplanted by the larger barrel churns which could be rapidly rotated by a foot pedal.

MILK-HOUSES

The plentiful stone found on the Canadian Shield was used by some German farmers to construct milk-houses, partly subterranean, where dairy products could be stored at cool temperatures.

STONE MILKHOUSE
This stone milkhouse was built by William Maves, son of a German immigrant, on the rocky ground of his farm in Alice Township. There was no shortage of building material for the second generation who tilled the land.

Built by Karl Hildebrandt who immigrated in 1873.

Built by Charles Greif c. 1900.

The priority that German immigrants placed on the keeping of swine may be judged by the choice of the animal that Mrs. August Kruger and her three sons took with them when they travelled to Krugerdorf in 1905. Making their way north, partly by train, partly by boat and partly on foot, in order to join August Kruger and his son, Frank, in Chamberlain Township, the mother and sons took with them a large sow, ready to farrow; unfortunately a bear made off with the pig on the first night that the animal spent in a pen in its new home. A similar tale is told of the fate of the pig kept by a Mr. Shurman, one of the pioneers at Petawawa; this pig-pen had been protected at night by the lighting of a fire, presumably to scare off any four-legged marauders. One night when no fire was lit the domestic animal was seized by a bear and partially devoured. When the bear returned three nights later, it was shot by Carl Gutzman who had been stationed in the hay loft for just this purpose. "To the dismay of these poor settlers they would have to wait a year or more for their much desired pork, and delicious sausages," wrote one chronicler of this event.

As Mr. French had remarked in his handbook of information for intending settlers, horses and sheep cannot well be supported unless there is some land cleared and laid down in pasture upon which they may graze. This assertion is confirmed by the figures given in the records of William Sinn, the agent who had visited the German farms in October, 1860. Wilhelm Schroder of South Algona Township, who had been settled on his land there since the spring of 1959 had cleared 11 acres and his assets included one cow, two young cattle and four sheep. Six other men who had come to South Algona Township from the same village as Schroder, Breitenstein, Friedeberg, Frankfurt-a-Oder, had but recently arrived, in the fall of 1860; they had not cleared any acres yet and did not own any livestock. These friends were: Friedrich Sell, John Bohn, Gottlieb Moller, Gottlieb Quast, August Schroder and Christian Quast. The most successful farmer appeared to be Martin Budarich Sr. who had cleared 36 acres since his arrival in the fall of 1858; upon his property were grazing two cows, two oxen, four young cattle and five sheep.

FOR SCALDING PIGS
The killing of livestock on the farms was conducted out of doors. One of the operations performed outside the house was the removal of hair and bristles from the slaughtered pigs by hot water. This scalding could be accomplished by a cauldron of water boiled over an open fire, into which the carcass could be dipped. On this German farm in North Algona Township the cauldron has been set in a permanent stand of concrete, with an entry for the fuel to be inserted beneath the container.

BACON AND HAM UNDER PREPARATION
Butchering pigs and preparing cuts of meat for the smokehouse is still an annual event practised by German families in Renfrew County. Walter Zadow tackles this job on a fine fall day out of doors on a farm in South Algona Township.

SAUSAGE-MAKING
Mrs. Walter Zadow is showing her young son how sausages are made. The ground pork has been mixed with seasonings and then the minced meat is pressed into metal grinders; the product is squeezed through a tube into casings, a thin-skinned container which is traditionally provided by the washed intestines of pigs.

SMOKEHOUSES (2)
In Wilberforce Township, Mrs. Adolph (Hertha) Ott keeps a supply of sawdust and rotted maple beside the smokehouse that was built in 1938 and which is used annually.

SMOKEHOUSES (1)
During the 1930s, Mr. and Mrs. William Lemke found that the preparation of sausages cured in their smokehouse was a more profitable way to market pork than to sell the pigs.

SMOKEHOUSES (3)
At this smokehouse on the farm of Mrs. John Luloff, there was a 'meat tree' from the limbs of which the carcasses of game could be hung. Grattan Township, on the shoreline of the Bonnechere River.

Budarich and many other of those early settlers from Germany had chosen Wilberforce Township in which to settle. Being one of the central townships in Renfrew County and one of the largest, it affords a good example of the mixture of ethnic groups that had decided to farm in this part of Canada by the time of the 1871 census. The most numerous residents were the Irish, 111 families that totalled 1,025 persons; second in numbers were the Germans, 60 families comprising 625 members. There were 16 households headed by Scots (179 people), eight described as English (69) and only four that were French. In that year, unlike 1861, the federal census-takers made notes on the "industrial establishments" that were operating in this eastern Ontario county where pioneer conditions prevailed. There were no advanced manufacturers in the region. The businesses that the census-takers found in the rural townships on the Canadian Shield reflected the scene of settlement in a new agricultural frontier; they found potash works, charcoal pits, lime kilns, and the home industries of artisans such as harness-makers, blacksmiths, shoe and boot-makers and weavers' shops.

Ralph Lett, the enumerator for Wilberforce Township in 1871, made extensive notes on the weaving of cloths and fabrics at home. He found that at least two-thirds of the farm families made their own textiles, producing their own yarn and weaving it themselves. It was one of the tasks that ensured self-sufficiency. Mr. Lett recorded the number of yards of cloth and flannel made from wool at each home and listed separately the yards of home-made linen. On separate pages he described those who were weaving in quantity for sale to others, and although these businesses were apparently owned by the husbands, the work was invariably done by the women.

Of the 320 households in that township in 1871, 199 produced home-made cloths and flannels using wool, but only 19 families were weaving linen from flax. Those who were not making their own textiles included some solitary bachelors and some families headed by widowers. There were some who were obviously related to weavers who produced enough for the extended family and there were others who must have comprised the customers for the four weaver's shops, two of which were owned by German immigrants, Friedrich Wolfgram and August Lang.

Whether their production was purely domestic or intended for sale, the weavers of Wilberforce Township (and other central townships in the county such as Grattan and the Algonas) had access to two carding and fulling mills, powered by the Bonnechere River at Eganville. Carding wool into rolls, performed by machinery, relieved the weaver of a messy and time-consuming job before the task of spinning the wool yarn. The mass of wool fibres was combed into a straight and parallel bundle.

The labours of the weavers were conducted only for part of the year, but they added significantly to the family's income. Eliza Wolfgram, 50, the German-born wife of Friedrich Wolfgram, earned $38 as her yearly wage for working four months and in that time produced 480

SMOKEHOUSES (4)
On an uninhabited farm in Grattan Township that once belonged to a family named Schmidt, an overhanging roof protects the entrance to a log smokehouse which is set into a bank of earth; this is a style reminiscent of German farms in Pennsylvania.

SMOKEHOUSES (5)
Beyond the smokehouse on this farm in Radcliffe Township, lies the uneven topography and stony soil of an area that is designated as Class 7 (unfit for agriculture). Log fences show where Martin Schweig, a stonemason who came here from Germany in 1882, cleared and used the land. He built his house of stone and the smokehouse was placed at a discreet distance.

yards of flannel valued at $384. The cost of the raw materials had been $150 for 240 lbs woollen yarn and $32 for cotton yarn, so the net profit for the weaver's shop was $204, less than the wage of the weaver. By the standards of 1871, this was quite a good yield for four months' work; there were schoolteachers in the rural townships of Renfrew County who had to be content with a salary of $200 to $300 for a year of teaching. The other German weaver in Wilberforce Township that year was Charlotte Lang, 46, whose wage for seven month's work was $56.

The output of the home looms varied from as little as 10 yards to as much as 120 yards in a year. There must have been factors such as the size of the family, the health of the mother or the success of the sheep-rearing that governed the amount of weaving that was accomplished in any one year; it was independent of any ethnic origin judging from the wide variance found in Wilberforce Township. Mr. Lett's careful records establish that the French families topped the list with an average of 59.2 yards per family, while the Germans came last with 33.1 yards average per household.

There was one type of weaving, however, in which the Germans were pre-eminent; the production of linen. Of the 19 households that manufactured cloth from flax, 17 were German, the other two Irish. There were some homes in which only flax was woven into cloth; these were the households of Gotlip Bramberger, William Biederman, August Burke, Martin Lebeck, Martin Budher and John Budder. These six families lived in the north-west corner of Wilberforce Township, near the village of Rankin and therefore close to the weaver's shop of August Lang.

FARMING IN RENFREW COUNTY HAS LIMITATIONS
Sheep, belonging to Adolph Ott of Wilberforce Township, are penned at night to protect them from wolves. Cattle, have to be sheltered and fed during the winter months when snow covers the ground.

The Eganville Leader. July 17, 1914.

WANTED
20,000 Pounds Washed Wool.

We will pay the highest Cash, Trade or Account Price for same. Bring us your wool and save money.

In the Grocery Line
Choice Lines Imported Evening Biscuits.   Choices Old Country Pure Jams.
Pure Maple Syrup 25c per qt. - the pure cannot be sold cheaper ; compound can be sold at 20c per qt.
Limited quantity of the finest Oranges.   15c per dozen.

Est. W. GEORGE
Eganville,   Ont.

WASHED WOOL WANTED
Before shearing a flock of sheep in early summer, a farmer might make some attempt to wash the woolly coats of the animals in a creek or pond. The wool of the sheep in some pastures was prickly with thorns or burrs and some merchants wanted this removed.

Because the majority of homes in Wilberforce Township in 1871 were places where cloth was produced by the family, there had to be tools such as spinning-wheels in all these homes to enable the women to make the yarn. There had to be wool-winders and swifts and bobbin-winders, in order that the spun yarn could be measured and wound and unwound on to bobbins before weaving took place. Some of these tools, such as the niddy-noddy or the flax hackles, were simple enough to be made by the individual farmer. The local carpenter might make the looms or the bobbin-winder, but it took a skilled woodworker to make a spinning-wheel. Fortunately for the daughters of the German immigrants there were several man who had the talent to make the wheels from local hardwoods in their new country.

Granddaughters of the immigrants are still using some of the spinning-wheels, women like Mrs. Rose Yeas of Pembroke who not only appears at exhibitions like the one at the Pembroke Legion, May 1, 1986, but who actually takes orders from those who want a home-knitted garment made from the natural sheep's wool. In the spring of 1986, Mrs. Yeas, the granddaughter of Wilhelm Ferdinand Brasch and Paulina Doering, 19th century immigrants, was making a sweater for a man in Ohio from brown sheep's wool that had not been dyed. Spinning and knitting the spun wool is an art that has not vanished among the German settlement in Renfrew County. Weaving is no longer practised on the huge looms to make cloth and the growing of flax was abandoned soon after the first world war.

SPINNING-WHEEL MADE IN RENFREW COUNTY
Spinning-wheels, like this one, that were made in Renfrew County by German immigrants from local hardwoods, have larger diameters and more spokes than similar styles brought from Germany. This wheel, with 16 spokes, was made by Christian Born of Alice Township for a relative. Christian Born (spelled Boorn) 45, appears on the 1871 census of that township, with his wife, Louisa, 39, and their two children, Anistina, 17 and William, 12, all born in Germany. The head of the household is listed as a farmer.

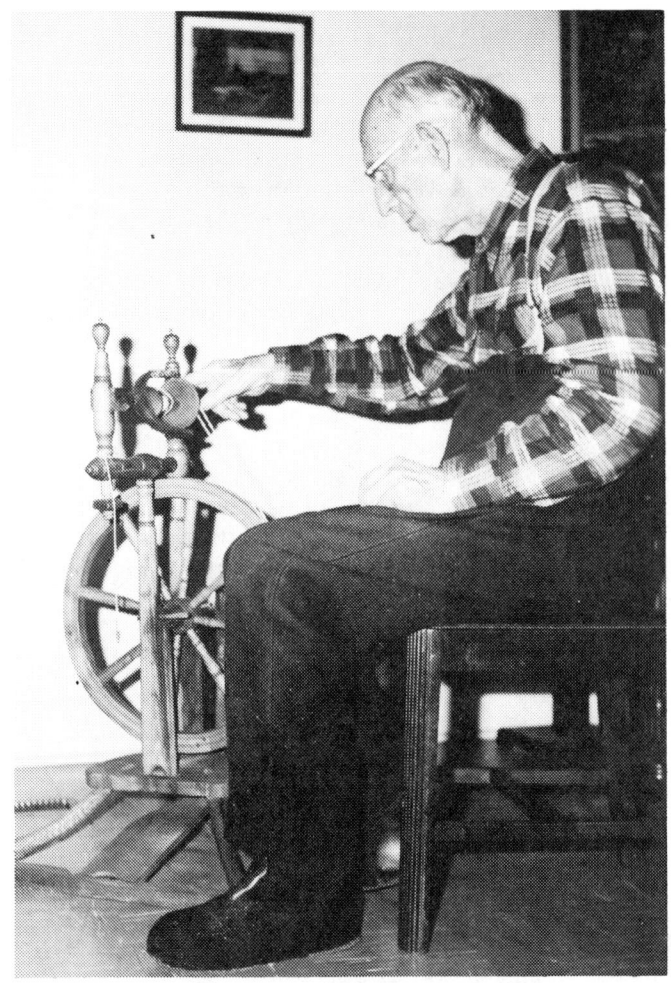

VERTICAL SPINNING-WHEEL MADE IN RENFREW COUNTY
Mr. Solomon Kelo of Wilberforce Township was photographed, Sept. 7, 1979, with one of the vertical or upright spinning-wheels that had been made by his grandfather, Martin Markus, who emigrated from Germany in 1863 and settled in Wilberforce Township. The same style of spinning-wheel was brought to Canada from Germany by some immigrants, such as Mrs. Matthew Horcun, who came from Drachausen, Cottbus, the same area that Martin Markus had left. The ones made by Markus are fashioned from black ash; the ones from Germany are made from other hardwoods.

SPINNING APPARATUS
A niddy-noddy (on the ground), a spinning-wheel, a box of bobbins and a barrel swift all emerged in a 1984 auction sale from the barns on a farm at Augsburg, which had once been owned by Charles Hoelke (1854-1936), a German immigrant who farmed and was skilled at making spinning-wheels for others in his workshop.
The barrel swift, rare in Renfrew County, gains its name from the revolving cages shaped like barrels that old the skeins of wool which are to be unwound. In this model, the intervals between the two cages could be changed. The cages are wide enough to hold two skeins, side by side, an arrangement that may have been useful when plying two strands of yarn.

VERTICAL SPINNING-WHEEL MADE IN GERMANY
When Mr. and Mrs. Gustave Michel packed their baggage for a journey to Canada in 1867, they brought most of this spinning-wheel with them. The upper portion of this wheel could be taken apart and the pieces compactly stored, but space was so restricted that the original stand and foot-pedal were left behind in Tuppendorf, Silesia. On arrival in Petawawa Township, the husband made a plain three-legged stand out of pine for the spinning-wheel which was re-assembled in its new home. Sheep were kept on the Michels' farm until the 1940s. This wheel was used by Mrs. Gustave Michel and subsequently by her daughter-in-law, Mrs. Robert Michel, who had ten children to clothe.
This style of vertical or upright spinning-wheel has been found on the prairie provinces among immigrants from Germany and the Ukraine, but it was also made in Renfrew County by a German immigrant for the second generation, the daughters of immigrants.

VERTICAL SPINNING-WHEEL FROM COTTBUS AREA (missing link)
Photographed on Easter weekend 1986 at a Hagarty Township farm, this vertical or upright spinning-wheel was brought from Drachausen, Cottbus, by Mrs. Matthew Horcun in 1863; it is in the possession of the third generation of the Okum family, whose surname has changed in spelling. The spinning-wheel has many similarities to the ones made in Renfrew County by Martin Markus, who also came from Drachausen, Cottbus, but the German one has six spokes instead of eight, the rim is broader and the wood is oak. The style of the base is almost a replica of the ones made by Markus, who probably copied a spinning-wheel brought from his area in Germany.

**ANOTHER MARKUS SPINNING-WHEEL,
AND WITH ATTACHED ARM**

This vertical spinning-wheel was found in 1986, in an attic of a farm in Petawawa Township that had belonged to the Schroeder family; its style is exactly the same as those known to have been made by Martin Markus, except for the extra arm. The owner, who knew that the Markuses and the Schroeders had been related, did not know what the function of the extra arm could have been; it might have held the hanks of carded wool that were to be drawn into spun thread.

SWIFT. (1)

Used for unwinding skeins of yarn, the X-shaped swift made by the German immigrants was a collapsible piece of equipment on a tall frame, from which it could be detached. This one on the farm of Wesley Budd, Budd Mills, Wilberforce Township, is typical and was probably used by the grandmother of the last owner, Mrs. Wilhelm Budd who left Germany and came to Renfrew County with her husband and four children in 1872. Swifts of this style commonly emerge at auction sales on German farms that have been owned by three successive generations of the same family. They were made to be used with the operator in a standing position, unlike the French-Canadian swifts found in Quebec which allow one to unwind skeins while seated. Holes in the arms of the swift accommodate different lengths of skeins to be used on it.

SWIFT. (2)
Similar in style to swift (1), this X-shaped device, which could be folded flat, lifted off its stand and stored away was made by Otto Lenser, son of a German immigrant. He was obviously copying the style made by the earlier German settlers in Renfrew County. It was sold by his son, Martin, at an auction sale in South Algona Township.

SIMPLE CLOCK REEL
The clock reel was more efficient than the niddy-noddy for winding or skeining wool, and it was a device that was produced commercially in Waterloo County, Ontario, by 1868. This specimen is obviously home-made. It was found in the attic of a German farm at Germanicus, Wilberforce Township, one that was being readied for an auction sale by the third generation from a German immigrant, Ernst Brose. One of the four arms of this reel bears a handle for the operator to clasp while turning. The reel has a sturdy stand, but no cogs or gears to measure the length of yarn.

COMPLICATED CLOCK REEL
The turning of this clock reel activates a couple of wooden gears. After 40 revolutions of the reel, a peg on the lower gear presses against a piece of wood attached to the rear post, causing it to click sharply. This noisy click indicates that 40 rounds of yarn have been wound. With six spokes shaped on a lathe, this finely-crafted reel was made by William Born of Alice Township, son of a German immigrant, Christian Born, who made spinning-wheels. The reel was made for a niece, Bertha Timm, and was later owned and used by a descendant's wife, (note the wool wound on it).

BOBBIN-WINDER

For weaving, the yarn had to be wound on spools for making the warp or on bobbins to fit into the shuttle. Either spools or bobbins were wound by placing them on a spindle in the box, turning the large drive wheel by hand and feeding it with the yarn from a skein of spun thread. In the bobbin-winders that are commonly found on the German farms in Renfrew County, the drive wheel has no rim; instead the spokes end in a T-shaped projection where the yarn is held in a concave depression. Stored away now in an attic or a barn, these bobbin-winders were once an essential aid for weaving cloth on a loom on the farm. The bobbins and shuttles and spools might be made in the wintertime by the children of the family, some decorated by incising them with a nail. The bobbin-winders, mounted on a sturdy stand, could be made by a skilled farmer or the local carpenter. This one was found in a barn in South Algona Township, where the original owners of the land were called Schultze.

Eganville Leader. May 27 - June 3, 1932.

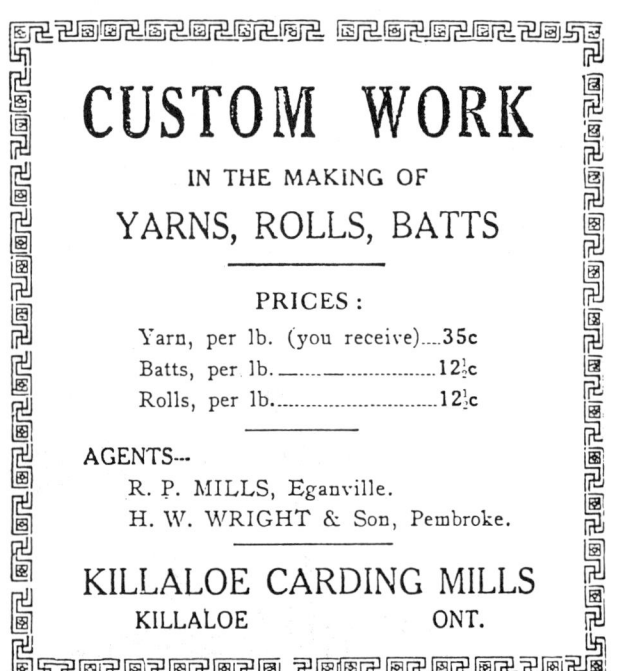

CUSTOM WORK
IN THE MAKING OF
YARNS, ROLLS, BATTS

PRICES:

Yarn, per lb. (you receive)....35c
Batts, per lb. 12½c
Rolls, per lb. 12½c

AGENTS---

R. P. MILLS, Eganville.
H. W. WRIGHT & Son, Pembroke.

KILLALOE CARDING MILLS
KILLALOE   ONT.

CARDING MILL. 1932.

At a time of year when fleeces would be sheared from the sheep, this mill at Killaloe advertised carding services. Raw wool from the farms could be combed here. Knitted socks, mitts and sweaters from homespun yarn were especially welcome during the years of the Depression. Wool was used to stuff quilts before synthetic fibres became available.

FLAX TOOLS

Although William Sinn, a government immigration agent who visited those German farmers who had settled on land by 1860, noted that eight German farmers had begun cultivation of flax within a couple of years of their arrival, the use of this plant fibre in the making of textiles ended during the lifetime of the second generation. Descendants of German immigrants, in the third or fourth generation, can barely remember the harvesting of flax or the tools that were needed for the preparation of linens. The flax-breaker, which crushed the dried stalks of the flax plants, and the hackles that teased the strands of the broken stalks and straightened out the wiry fibres, were found in a barn in Petawawa Township, where a family of German descent had lived for over a century. No one could recall their use.

SAUERKRAUT-MAKING

It's a family affair when the Schauers get together to make sauerkraut. In a Cobden kitchen the distaff side cut up the cabbages before a couple of men take their turn at the sauerkraut cutter.

HOME-MADE SAUERKRAUT CUTTER

Made by William Klingbeil, Wilberforce Township, this sauerkraut cutter has a lid which was used to compress the shredded cabbage in the box. The blades have been taken from scythes or reapers.

NONAGENARIAN QUILTING

Mrs. Adolph Grife, known affectionately to everybody as "Granny Grife", was busy quilting at her home in Rankin, Wilberforce Township, May 14, 1980, in her 92nd year. Born Elizabeth Sell, the daughter of Fritz Sell and Gusta Ott, she was married to Adolph Grife in 1908 and widowed in 1960. Even in her 90s, "Granny Grife" maintained her independence, in her own home, close to the sawmill which her husband had operated.

COLOURFUL COTTON QUILTS

These two quilts and the afghan were made by Theresa Mueller who married William Verch in 1913. Patterns such as Sunbonnet Sue were widely available by 1920 and cotton fabrics were commonly used. The filling of the quilts was still wool and the stitching of some appliqued patterns such as Morning Glory was a display of skill.

Chapter IV.

Furnishing the home

Although most of the handmade furniture that has been retained from the self-sufficient farmhouses of the pioneers from Germany is pine, some of the finest pieces were made from black ash. From available literature, it would appear that Renfrew County is the only region in Canada where this hardwood was used for primary purposes in furniture. The discovery that a substantial amount of antique furniture in the United States was made of black ash, was described in the March/April 1985 issue of **Fine Woodworking** magazine by Jon W. Arno. He wrote that antique dealers and the general public often mistake this attractive, open-grained wood for oak, and he showed the difference between the two woods, the oak having prominent rays when it is cut radically or tangentially. It was his opinion that while three species of ash are suitable for cabinet woods (and all three grow in Renfrew County), the black ash (Fraxinus nigra) is the choice of the connoisseur.

An amateur woodworker himself, Mr. Arno of Brookfield, Wisconsin, wrote that the black ash, which is native to the Great Lake States, New England and Canada, typically grows in a harsh environment. The slow growth of the trees in such areas produces a high ratio of heartwood to sapwood, resulting in a wood that is lighter in weight, more porous and more interesting in figure. He did not consider that the black ash could ever rival the most highly-regarded cabinetwoods, such as rosewood, walnut, cherry or teak, but in their absence it provides an attractive alternative, combining strength relative to its weight and the amount of energy needed to shape it.

Black ash was used by at least four identifiable professional furniture-makers in Renfrew County. Examples exist of articles made in black ash by August Boehme (1841-1907), Friedrich August Gutzeit (1849-1926), Julius Albert Zadow (1854-1941) and Johann Friedrich Wilhelm Luloff (1859-1939). The three first-named were known to have been trained as furniture-makers in their native land before immigrating; the fourth one learned his skills from older men in the Golden Lake area, whose names cannot be learned. Searching through old census records in the hopes of identifying furniture-makers is unrewarding, for even if the man, such as Gutzeit, is known to have been skilled in this work, his occupation may be described as carpenter.

In the 1871 census records of Alice and Fraser townships, the only German immigrant named as a carpenter was Frederick Wiessenberg (1834-1910), whose descendants only know of his renown at making windmills. By the standards of that time, the modest woodworking business of this immigrant was listed as "an industrial establishment" and the details were recorded for posterity. Wiessenberg's fixed capital investment was $25. It was stated that he worked for four months of the year, using 500 feet of lumber, valued at $4. In that time he produced five tables and four cupboards, by hand work, and assessed their worth at $23. Wiessenberg died at the age of 75 years, in 1910, having never been fit enough to farm because of wounds that he received while serving in the Union Army in the American Civil War. If he worked for only a few months each year as a furniture-maker, his small output could have supplied tables and cupboards for nearby farms from 1863 until his death. The enumerator commented that Wiessenberg "works out amongst the farmers", suggesting that the furniture was made when a customer placed an order. This agrees well with the stories heard about the trade conducted by other furniture-makers in the rural townships, who did some work at home and some on the premises of the customers. The same was true of tailors and weavers and gunsmiths. There were no large manufacturing enterprises established in the countryside by German immigrants who had these skills, probably because there was insufficient population to warrant factory-scale production in Renfrew County. By 1911, the total population was only 47,443 in 3,009 square miles.

Working in isolation, the German immigrants produced their basic furnishings from the native woods with various degrees of competence. There are very few items that bear any identification of the person who made them. If the furniture-maker moved away, died young or had no descendants, the puzzle of identity may never be solved. Identification is even more difficult once the piece has passed through several hands on its way to the antique store or museum, and pickers have been scouring the farms in this German settlement since the 1960s.

When the most backbreaking years were behind them, the German immigrants could afford to make their surroundings more comfortable and decorative. Few had brought any musical instruments with them, and the purchase of an organ, which acted as a focus for family entertainment, was obviously popular. There was no tradition of handpainted birth certificates or embroidered show towels among the immigrants from north-eastern Germany. There was, however, a considerable market for embroidered pictures, which bore messages in the German language praising the virtues of a godly home. These framed pieces of needlework, which are sometimes highlighted by a celluloid figure in the guise of an angel or Jesus Christ, are found in old homes which have been occupied by a German family for three or more generations. They seem to date from the last decade of the 19th century and no one can remember how they were acquired. Because so many turn up in farms in townships that are far from towns, there is some speculation that they were sold door to door by travelling salesmen.

The black and white sketches of the first and second generation were also framed and hung on the wall, but this is common to all the ethnic groups that had pioneered on the soil of eastern Ontario, not just the German people. Photographs that show interiors of homes in the lifetime of the first generation are rare, but one that was taken at Christmastime in the home of Carolina and Ferdinand Biesenthal, who raised 13 children, portrays a family that looks well-dressed and contented.

The ability to carve wood was enjoyed by several immigrants, some of whom have left behind evidence of their skill. An immigrant in Chalk River who carved animals, Charles August Vollgrath, who immigrated from Germany to Canada in 1892, was one whose work decorated the homes of friends and neighbours; in later years, he found that this skill could supplement his income when he sold his wares from a roadside stand to the motoring public during the Depression. Most men who carved in wood made objects only for their family, useful objects like a boot-jack, toys such as a rocking-horse and tests of skill like making a round ball within a squared cage. They have left a legacy of craftsmanship for others to admire.

CRADLE MADE FROM BLACK ASH
The head-board of this box-like cradle is decorated with an incised design that includes a rosette, a characteristic German motif; otherwise the four sides of panelled black ash are plain.

CLOTHES CUPBOARD MADE FROM BLACK ASH
This tall clothes cupboard, with lamb's tongue corners, is topped by a cornice that has black and gold painted designs on wood that is probably basswood. Most of the cupboard is constructed from black ash and the grain of the wood is sufficient decoration for it was not covered by paint. The interior of the cupboard has two rows of fixed pegs at the top, made from pine, to hold clothes; the single drawer at the base could have been used to store blankets. This cupboard, which looks like the work of a skilled man, was made for Bertha Frietag who lived near Golden Lake in a two-storey farmhouse. It was sold by a granddaughter at an auction sale in 1983.

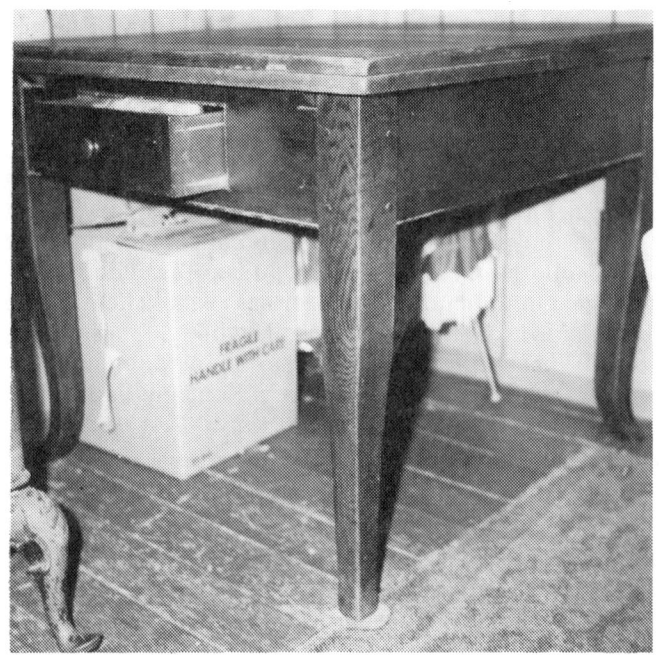

TABLE MADE FROM BLACK ASH
The draw-leaf extension table has been found in Ontario only in regions where German immigrants settled, for example, in Waterloo County. In Renfrew County, this style is also found in the homes of German immigrants, sometimes square (as this one) and sometimes rectangular in shape. This table has a single dovetailed drawer on the same side as an extension leaf, a curious position because the drawer would be difficult of access once the leaf is extended. The legs have an outward curve at the end, a feature which is also believed to be a characteristic of German work. This table was in use by the third generation from a German immigrant, by Elmer Maves in Alice Township who had inherited it from his father. He did not know who had made it. This type of table was produced by trained furniture-makers such as Fred Gutzeit of South Algona Township and also by individual craftsmen such as Ferdinand Biesenthal of Alice Township. Mr. Maves' table was destroyed when his house burned down.

WILLIAM FICK MADE A WASHING MACHINE FROM BLACK ASH

Of all the furnishings made by German immigrants in Renfrew County, this washing machine made from black ash by William Fick is probably one-of-a-kind. William Frederick Fick and his wife Dorothea had two sons, Gustave and William who were born in Germany. The second William Fick, who married Christiana Albertina Sterndorf and fathered six children, is believed to have been the builder of this washing machine; the couple were married c. 1875 and lived on a farm adjacent to his parents in Wilberforce Township. Some members of the fourth generation continue to live in this township. One has preserved the body of the washing machine as a handy container for logs by the fireside; another has the portrait of the man who made it.

CLOTHES CUPBOARD OF BLACK ASH

Under the varnish that had been applied to this cupboard could be seen the grain of black ash, and possibly some oak as well. The three-lobed decoration at the top was typical of some of the cupboards that were made by Bill Luloff of Golden Lake (1859-1939), such as the one he made for his niece, Sarah, in 1915. Since this cupboard came from a farm near Golden Lake, the similarity in shape in the cornice and overall style of the two-doored cupboard with fixed pegs inside and a single bottom drawer suggests that it may have been Luloff's work.

On opposite page:

CHEST OF DRAWERS MADE FROM BLACK ASH

This chest of drawers, made from black ash, has fine detail in the corners and the shaped feet. It came from the farm in Wilberforce Township that was owned in the 19th century by William Druve, father-in-law of a furniture-maker, John Kelo, who lived in a field beside his wife's family. Kelo died in the 1890s and his widow remarried and moved away.

HEART AND TWO EARS OF WHEAT
Black ash was used for a strong and heavy clothes cupboard that emerged from an auction at Budd Mills in 1983. The owner, Wesley Budd, said that the cupboard had come from Sam Liebeck's farm on the Marsh Road in Wilberforce Township about 20 years earlier, and relatives of the Liebeck family believed that it had been made by one of their antecedents. The symbols of a heart and two ears of wheat, supposedly representing love, prosperity, appear frequently on hand-made cupboards at German homes, whether they were made by a skilled man or an amateur. Carving on a softwood such as pine or basswood is easier than attempting to carve these symbols on black ash, as on this one.

Streseman family, Alice Township.

STICK STOOLS
Surely the simplest of all the basic furnishings that German immigrants made for their new homes in the wilderness must have been these slab seats with splayed legs. They turn up with surprising frequency at auction sales, and usually nobody can remember who made them.

Budd family, Wilberforce Township.

BLACK ASH USED BY THIRD GENERATION
Construction of functional furniture by those who had no formal training continued to be a tradition in some German families. Edmund Verch of Pembroke (grandson of Louis F. Verch and August Mueller) made furniture from black ash in the 1930s and 1940s, for use in the large kitchens of his sisters' farmhouses. This is a kitchen bench, with hinged seat, that he made from hardwood on the family farm in South Algona Township.

Wilberforce Township. On the farm of Karl Hildebrandt who emigrated 1873.

STICK STOOLS
North Algona Township. On the farm of Johann Luloff who emigrated 1867. A crude seat in which four splayed legs enter a single board.

PLAIN KITCHEN TABLE
With tapering handmade squared legs that are attached to the skirt of the table with wooden pegs, with several boards forming the surface of the table and with one small drawer, this was the sort of plain kitchen table that the average home handyman could make with a few tools. From the home of Johann Krohn, Germanicus, Wilberforce Township, a farmer mentioned in the 1881 census.

SPINDLE-BACK WINDSOR CHAIR
Stripped of its paint, this chair has a plank seat made of pine. The posts, spindles, legs and stretchers are made of ash. The maker is believed to have been August Kirsch. August and his wife, Augusta, emigrated to Canada with three children born in Germany. The census-taker of 1881 recorded the family's name as Kirk.

DOLL'S CRADLE MIMICS BABY'S CRADLE
The doll's cradle made by Ferdinand Biesenthal of Alice Township (above) has four posts, spindled sides and crescent-shaped rockers at the ends, just like the baby's cradle from the home in Wilberforce Township where it had rocked three generations of Kelos.

DOLL'S CRADLE
Made of pine in the box-like Germanic style with deep rockers, cradle (above) was made by Fred Yandt in 1910 for a daughter. Cradle (below) with dolls in it was made by Adolph Grife for his sister, Emma, in 1903; in 1980 Emma (Mrs. Raymond Ashick) kept the cradle to entertain visiting grandchildren. Both in Wilberforce Township.

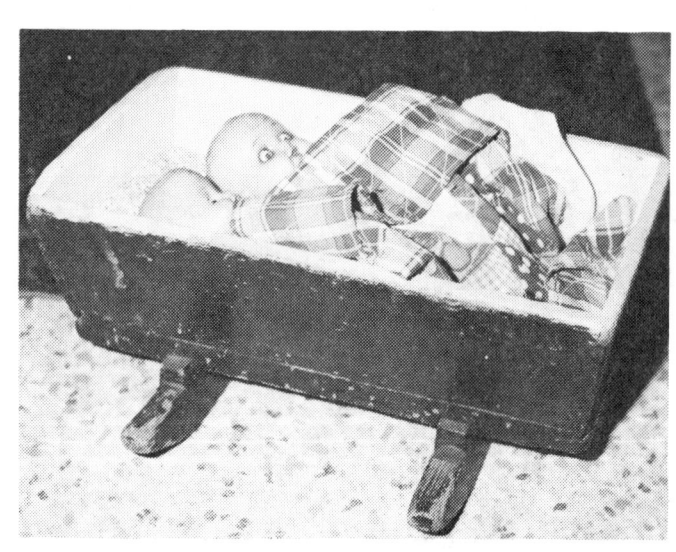

BED WITH PANELLED HEADBOARD AND FOOTBOARD
Though this style of bed has been described as Polish, it was a style made by several German furniture-makers, including Carl Gutzman of Petawawa Township (1850-1936) and Friedrich August Gutzeit of South Algona Township (1849-1926). Both these immigrants came from Pomerania where German and Polish people lived in close proximity.

SWINGING CRADLE
An uncommon style in any part of Ontario, this swinging cradle is believed to have been made by Louis Frederick Verch, who emigrated from Germany to eastern Ontario in the 1870s and had ten children. The cradle is owned by his descendants and is occasionally used.

DISCARDED PAIL-BENCH
The pail-bench at this farm in Budd Mills was in use until the 1950s when hydro-electric power lines reached the home, at the end of a mile-long driveway. Water pumped from a well was stored in buckets on this bench in the kitchen. Without electricity it was not feasible to install an indoor water supply. Five coats of paint on this pail-bench showed that it had been useful for several generations.

THE FOUR-POSTER BED
A lathe was necessary to make turned posts, and it was a skilled man who could make four posts in the same style. This four-poster, made from pine, was fashioned by a German from West Prussia who emigrated at the age of 46, with his wife and four sons, settling in Petawawa Township. Photographed in 1980, the bed was still in use by a grandson.

SIMPLE PAIL-BENCH
When August Boehme transferred his 200-acre farm in Raglan Township to his son and daughter-in-law, in March 1905, he had already built and furnished a small retirement home for his second wife and himself where they could live in independence. In this wooden, two-storey dwelling, one corner of the kitchen contained a pail-bench with one shelf. Pail-benches made for a family usually have two or three shelves.

AMATEUR'S FOOD CUPBOARD

Useful because of their shelves, food cupboards have often been kept by families long after the farm has been sold and the descendants have moved to an urban centre. This food cupboard was used by Mrs. Carl Schultze on a farm in Germanicus, Wilberforce Township, and is owned by a granddaughter who lives in Pembroke.

MADE ON THE PETAWAWA PLAINS — MILCHSCHRANK

One of the most utilitarian pieces of furniture was the "milchschrank" or milk cupboard, for the storage of foods and especially dairy products. This was a cupboard with sturdy shelves enclosed by doors to protect the contents. Though it might be placed in a basement or a stone-walled shed, close to the house, this cupboard made by skilled and unskilled woodworkers of German origin often had a decorative gallery (at the top) and a scrolled skirt (along the bottom). This one was made by August Gust who located on a farm in Petawawa Township, c. 1888, where he made his home furnishings from pine. When his married son and family had to leave the farm, because the Dept. of Militia and Defence bought them out, they took their personal effects from their home to a new farm in Alice Township. Descendants have them still.

FOOD CUPBOARD

Painted to match the surrounding walls of the living room, this pine food cupboard (with replaced pulls) continues to serve a useful function in the lives of the fourth generation to live in this house. Maker unknown. North Algona Township.

THE RANKIN FOOD CUPBOARD
Whoever made this style of food cupboard, double-doored with vertical bars that allow ventilation, reproduced a traditional form found in northern Germany. The pediment on this one is plain and not typical; usually the top has a scalloped or curved outline. These food cupboards are found on German farms in the Rankin region, in the northwest corner of Wilberforce Township. This one was offered for sale at an antique show in Kingston in 1980.

FOOD CUPBOARD WITH WHEAT MOTIF
This one-piece food cupboard, made from pine for a German family named Krohn in the rural community of Germanicus, has the symbol of a sheaf of wheat at the summit. The growing of wheat was once considered so important that samples of Canadian wheat were shown to prospective immigrants in Germany, as proof that the land offered in Renfrew County was fertile. Wheat-growing in eastern Ontario gradually lost favour when the western provinces began producing this grain. This food cupboard, with its useful shelves, was photographed in the possession of a granddaughter of Johann Krohn.

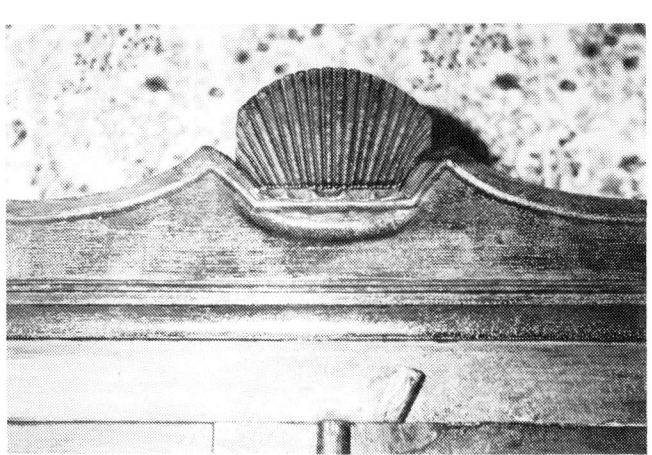

73

OPEN DRESSER

Open dressers were much less common in the German homes of Eastern Ontario than the kitchen cupboards which had glazed doors enclosing the shelves. This one was made by Johann Gotlieb Lipke, who was not a furniture-maker, but an accomplished immigrant from Neu Collatz, who came to Canada in 1863 and eventually secured his Crown Grant in 1874 in Germanicus. Some of the pine furniture that he made for his one-and-a-half-storey farmhouse, occupied by three generations of his family, was sold at a yard sale, August 29, 1980. The panelled chamfered doors of this cupboard still bore traces of yellow and blue paint.

KITCHEN CUPBOARD ABANDONED

The fate of many a cupboard, handmade by the pioneers from Germany, is to end up in a field, exposed to the elements and the highest bidder. Originally this kitchen cupboard was in the home of the Blemkie family, one of the few German families of the Roman Catholic faith who settled in the Mt. St. Patrick parish near the Ottawa and Opeongo Road, before the end of the 19th century. This cupboard had been inherited by a descendant who had moved to a farm in Ross Township. It was sold there at an auction sale, April 26, 1980, when the last owners were preparing to move to Toronto. Typical of German work, this cupboard had a pediment, an arched section attached to the top or cornice. It was made from pine.

KITCHEN IN A CENTURY FARM

The kitchen in this log farmhouse built in 1865 by an immigrant from West Prussia shows a combination of the old and the new. Beside the freezer-refrigerator there is a tall and venerable flat-to-the-wall pine cupboard, so old that its date and origin are unknown; its shelves, drawers and cupboard space are still in use by the third generation of the family who live here. Beside the electric stove is a dough-box, no longer employed for bread-making, but useful for storage.

DISH CUPBOARD BY A SKILLED MAN

Made from pine, this glazed cupboard displays a number of features that reveal the skill of a trained furniture-maker. The arched cornice with its central fan at the summit, is a style that has been considered to be Polish, identified with the Wilno area in Renfrew County, but it was a style that was used by expert German furniture-makers too. This cupboard was made for a German immigrant, Julius Haas of Locksley, Alice Township, and is in the possession of a granddaughter. It was probably made by Johann Noack, (1839-1919) a skilled furniture-maker in that German Lutheran community, an immigrant who came to Canada in 1869 from Frankfurt.

TWO DETACHED KITCHEN CUPBOARDS OFFERED FOR SALE

Detached from their original homes, these free-standing cupboards were offered for sale in 1982. They had come from farms which had been in the same family since the 1881 census.

Made by Julius Yake, Brudenell Township.

From the Runtz farm, Lyndoch Township.

The plain blanket chest made from pine and dovetailed at the corners was made by R.G. Reinke, who emigrated to Eganville in 1887 and began a lumbering business in partnership with two other men in 1895. This chest was made for a family in Wilberforce Township.

BLANKET CHESTS
Blanket chests in Ontario made from six boards are generally dated as pre-1870, but in Eastern Ontario the six-board chest was still being made in the 20th century by German woodworkers. Chests for use in the home (as opposed to travelling chests) were lifted off the floor by feet.

SIMPLE WASHSTAND
Relegated to the attic of a century-old farmhouse in Wilberforce Township, this plain washstand made from pine no doubt served its purpose when there was no indoor plumbing and water was supplied to individual bedrooms. The splashboard at the back protected the wall from careless users of the washing facilities.

The blanket chest made from black ash boards, edged and decorated with cedar, was constructed by Solomon Kelo, who was born in 1898 and lived in Wilberforce Township.

CORNER CUPBOARDS
Corner cupboards were not among the regular items made by skilled furniture-makers from Germany in eastern Ontario. Some were built into rooms or were constructed to be free-standing by house carpenters or home handymen and the styles vary. The massive glazed corner cupboard has been in its present home during the occupation of three generations. The small hanging corner cupboard, with only one original shelf, was nailed into a corner of the summer kitchen, before the last owners of the farm moved to a more modern home and discarded it.

The large corner cupboard is in North Algona Township and the small one was made for a farm in Wilberforce Township.

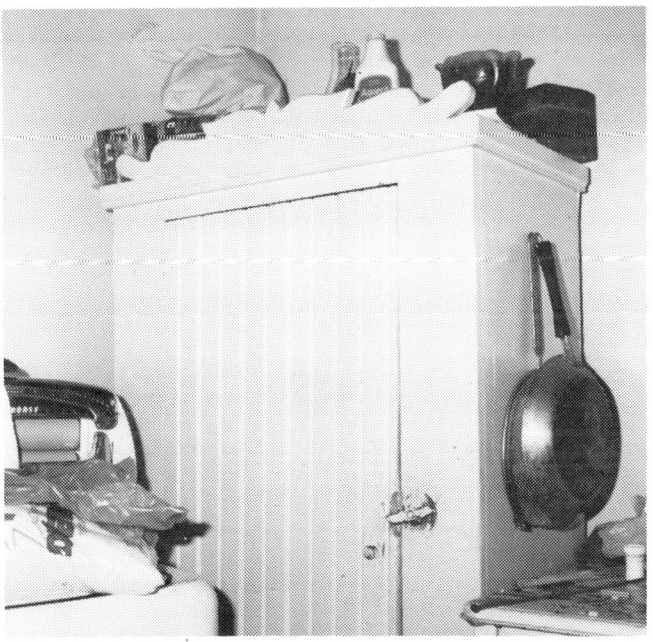

On opposite page:

WASHSTAND IN THE MINISTER'S ROOM
In one German farm that has 20th century comforts, including a modern bathroom, the room that was once reserved for the exclusive use of a visiting minister had been maintained in much the same style. One of the handmade furnishings was the washstand, fashioned from pine and decorated with a gallery at the back and a scalloped apron at the base.

In the days before indoor plumbing became common, the provision of a washstand in the bedroom, and its associated utensils for personal cleanliness, ensured privacy. Bars at the sides held towels, while the pieces of china on top contained water for washing, shaving and dental care; the cupboard may have been used to conceal a chamber pot.

IN THE FURNITURE-MAKER'S HOME
August Boehme (1841-1907), an immigrant from Germany, worked as a furniture-maker in several townships in Renfrew County, before settling down on land in Raglan Township to farm in 1874. He furnished his own home and made several pieces for his children's homes. In later life he built his own retirement home on the same property, still displaying the skill that had earned him a living (1865-1874) during his first years in eastern Ontario.

A decorative detail, sometimes termed a tulip motif, crowns the fretwork on this food cupboard made by Boehme and is echoed on the lintel above the door that leads from the kitchen to the bedroom in his retirement home.

ZADOW FURNITURE IDENTIFIED BY RELATIVES
J. Albert Zadow, photographed with his second wife, Auguste Ernestine Michaelis, whom he married in 1899, and the 17th child of his first marriage, Louise Auguste, born in 1898, was a trained furniture-maker who made many pieces for relatives. He had come to Canada in 1881, with his widowed mother and three brothers. All the brothers married and Albert made furniture for William, Edward and August, as well as for his own home and adult children.

August Zadow was a wagon-maker who lived in Eganville, where his house still stands on the Bonnechere River. It was there that a daughter, Gertrude, and a son, Eddie, identified this clothes cupboard as the work of Albert Zadow; the only change that has been made is the addition of pulls to the bottom drawer.

CUPBOARD MADE BY CARL GUTZMAN. (1850-1936)
Clothes cupboard made from pine by Carl Gutzman has fixed pegs inside at the top and a false drawer at the base. It is owned by a granddaughter of William Gutzman in Petawawa Township. William was one of three brothers who emigrated from Germany to Petawawa Township, where he worked as a tailor. Carl, who followed his older brothers, was a furniture-maker; his name appears on the assessment rolls in 1871, but he did not clear land in the first two years or own any livestock, which confirms that he was not farming.

BILL LULOFF, FURNITURE-MAKER AT GOLDEN LAKE
Johann Frederick Wilhelm "Bill" Luloff was only a child when he emigrated to Renfrew County from Falkenwalde, Pomerania, with his parents in 1867. Learning from other German woodworkers, he was a builder of wagons, coffins and furniture, which he made at a workshop in the village of Golden Lake. Portrait of Bill Luloff, who died in 1939.
Photograph courtesy Miss Teresa Luloff, Golden Lake.

The log building at Golden Lake, which was used as a workshop by Bill Luloff.

LULOFF CRADLE MADE FOR NIECE
Miss Teresa Luloff is holding a doll's cradle made for her by an uncle, furniture-maker Bill Luloff of Golden Lake.

FURNITURE-MAKER'S CHEST OF TOOLS
Frederick August Gutzeit (1849-1926), a trained furniture-maker, brought a chest of tools with him when he emigrated to Canada in 1874. This pine chest and its contents were inherited by his nephew, William Gutzeit, born in 1893, seen here with one of his uncle's planes. Mr. Gutzeit owned cupboards made by the furniture-maker who used pine in his early years and black ash at a later period.

KITCHEN CUPBOARD MADE BY ADOLPH GRIFE
One of the few German furniture-makers who used oak was Adolph Grife (1875-1960) of Rankin, Wilberforce Township. He made kitchen cupboards such as this one in the years before the First World War. This cupboard, which had been painted white, came from the home of Mrs. Adolph Grife, having been discarded when her kitchen was modernized and given to a neighbour.

SIDEBOARD BY ADOLPH GRIFE
Although the ability and the need to make furniture at home continued into the second generation of German families, the influence of catalogues, which showed illustrations of factory-made furniture, is reflected in some of the styles that were made. This sideboard was made of oak by Adolf Grife (1875-1960), the son of an immigrant, and the owner of the Rankin sawmill in Wilberforce Township from 1919 until the 1940 s.

THE ORGAN
The stands which once held oil lamps now hold potted plants, but even in the television age the organ occupies a prominent position in the living-room of many old farms in Renfrew County. The German immigrants were fond of music; one of them, Karl Schultze ("Musikant" Schultze of Alice Township) brought his violin from Germany with him and organized the first band in Pembroke. Some of the grandchildren of the immigrants remember that music was the chief source of entertainment in the home and many evenings were spent in learning how to play the organ. Large organs such as this one were popular in the farmhouses of Renfrew County in the last quarter of the 19th century. In the 1870s, factories in Toronto, Hamilton and Guelph, as well as small establishments in London, Woodstock and Bowmanville were advertising "every size and description of Church and Chamber Organs, with all the modern improvements and in the best possible style".

GERMAN PICTURES
This embroidered picture hung in a farmhouse in Petawawa Township during the lifetime of three generations of a German family. A translation of the message reads: "Have delight in the Lord who will give thee what thy heart desires".

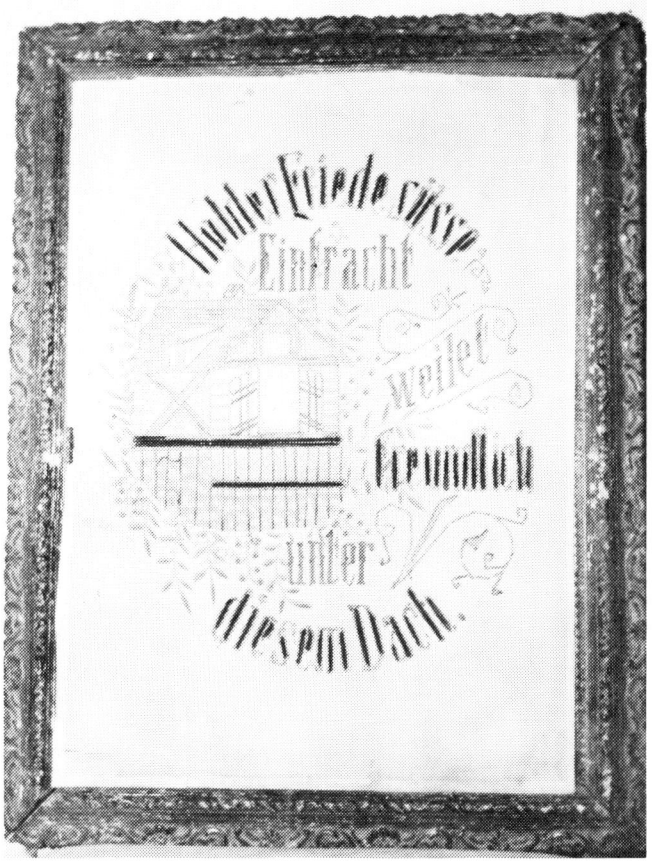

GERMAN PICTURES
This embroidered picture came from a German home in Pembroke. A translation of the message reads: "Sweet togetherness rests peacefully under a happy roof".

PIOUS PICTURE
Framed needlework pictures, bearing a message in the German language that refers to happiness in a home that is devout, once hung on the walls of some German homes in Eastern Ontario. Embroidered and appliqued on perforated paper, these pictures include a small attached figure of Christ, or an angel which is made of celluloid, and a decoration of feathery leaves which may be edelweiss. The message on this one — Gruss Gott tritt ein bring Luck herein — literally translates as Great God tread in bring Luck herein. According to the German National Museum at Nurnburg, these pictures were made in the late 19th century and were mainly popular with the lower middle class, both farmers and workmen. In Canada these pictures were owned by the first generation of immigrants but the origin is obscure; there seems to be no evidence that they were made in Canada and one owner suggested that they were sold door-to-door and came from the United States. From a farmhouse in Germanicus, Wilberforce Township.

Translation: "The highest fortune, the most beautiful joy is a beloved family life".

81

THE CHRISTINK FAMILY GROUP INCLUDED A MOOSE CARVING IN 1912

The farm of Irving Christink (bearded man on the right) was in Alice Township, close to the town of Pembroke and close enough for a professional photographer to visit the farm in 1912 to take pictures of a daughter's wedding. Other, less formal photographs appear to have been taken in the same period, such as this line-up of family members in front of the ivied log farmhouse.

At the right of the picture, the carving of a moose has been placed on a tree stump. One descendant of Irving Christink, who was not born when this photograph was taken, recalled that the carving had been made by a German immigrant in Chalk River called Vollrath. The owner of the carving rescued it from the farmhouse before it was demolished.

Photograph reproduced courtesy Lorne Christink.

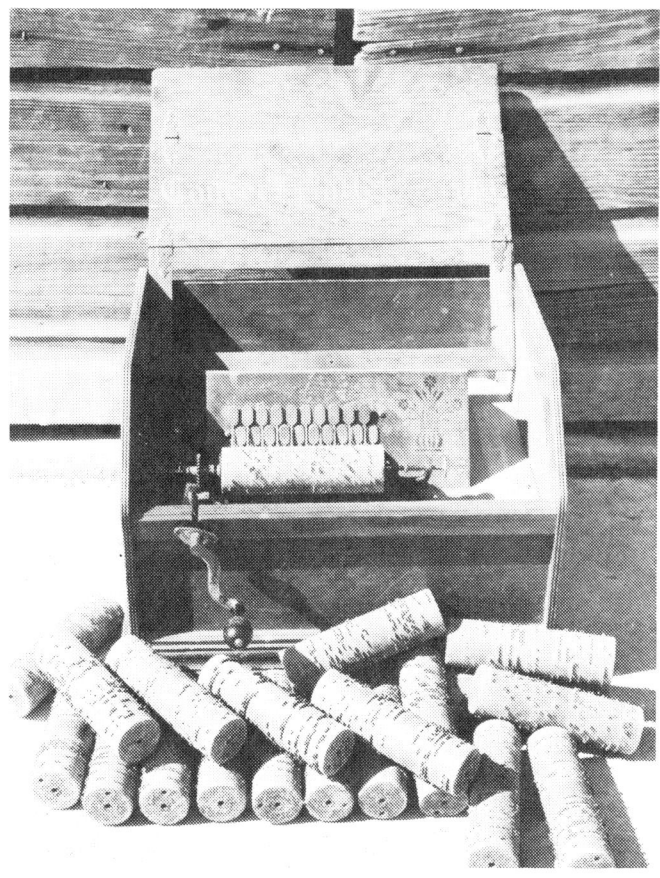

CONCERT ROLLER ORGAN
Made in Germany in the late 19th century (according to the patent inscription), this small organ supplied secular and religious music in farmhouses of modest size. This compact music box, with its repertoire of rollers, ended its career in a barn; the log house in which it provided music was demolished in the 1930s. In the 'second' log house there was space for the larger type of home organ.

Sold at a yard sale, Oct. 11. 1980. $100.

CHRISTMAS SCENE.
Married October 9, 1873, Ferdinand and Carolina Biesenthal were both born in Germany and came to Canada as young children. Seven daughters and six sons were brought up in the Biesenthal home in Alice Township, where the German language and German customs were maintained.
In this rare indoor photograph, believed to have been taken in 1916 or 1917, the elderly parents, seated in the centre, are shown with some of their children admiring Christmas presents in a setting that suggests comfort. The black and white sketch of the Biesenthal couple, probably done in the 1890s, can be seen on the wallpapered wall behind the family group.
There was no lack of evergreen trees in Eastern Ontario and the making of paper flowers and chains from coloured paper was a tradition that continued.

WEDDING CUPBOARD MADE FROM BLACK ASH
The tradition of the wedding cupboard, a piece of furniture made for a newly-married couple, continued for three generations in some German families. This one was made in 1938, by the bride's brother, from hardwood cut on the family's farm in South Algona Township. (The National Museum of Man in Ottawa has a German wedding cupboard from Renfrew County with a date of 1927 on it.) This glazed cupboard made from black ash has several characteristics that mark it as German work: the trio of compartments above, the trio of drawers below and the deep pie shelf.

Chapter V.

Signs of Change

In 1888, thirty years after the first German immigrants had arrived in eastern Ontario, the following advertisement was published in The Pembroke Observer.

German Night School

Rec. C. Schroeder, pastor of the Lutheran Church, Pembroke, begs to announce that he will begin evening classes in the Public School, early in October, for instruction in the German language. Pupils will be taught to speak, read and write German. The classes will meet twice a week, from 7.30 to 9 o'clock. This will be an excellent opportunity for English grown-up people and children and German grown-up people and children to acquire a knowledge of the German language. All children belonging to my own congregation will be admitted free.

Terms — One Dollar Per Month, In Advance.

Those intending to become pupils will please call at once at my house, close to the Lutheran church, Cemetery street, west end, Pembroke, where they can obtain full particulars. Please call either Tuesday or Thursday evening of any week, as on other evenings I am absent.

Pembroke. Sept. 14, 1888.   Rev. C. Schroeder

Rev. Conrad Schroeder had served the Lutheran Church of the Canada Synod at Green Lake, Wilberforce Township, before being installed as pastor of the Pembroke parish, Oct. 5, 1887. He must have noticed a difference in the use of German language in everyday conversation in his new urban parish, even though his church maintained the services wholly in the German tongue. His attempts to encourage the survival of the language spoken by the immigrants from Germany would not have been necessary in the rural townships. There, the German language would remain dominant in the lives of the German immigrants throughout the 19th century and prove to be a stumbling-block to education in the 20th century. Its survival was encouraged by the institution of 'German schools', conducted by the local German-speaking pastor, which caused the children to be absent from the public schools on certain days of the week. Then too, there was the problem of the distances children had to travel to get to school: truancy was heightened by the demands for the children to assist on the family farm.

Inspector R. George Scott who toured the one-roomed rural school in Renfrew County from 1877 to 1908, never ceased in his efforts to upgrade the educational facilities, but he admitted at the start of his stewardship:

"As many townships in this county contain a large amount of broken and poor land, and a consequently scattered population, the formation of school sections is attended with great difficulty... Teachers in our rural sections especially have little opportunity for meeting and exchanging ideas with those engaged in the same profession. They have few incentives around them to intellectual activity." Described by those who remember him as a 'gentleman of the old school', this inspector had been a high school teacher before he began his remarkable 30 years of travelling around the couty's 130 rural schools. He used horse and buggy or horse and cutter for many journeys, since the two railways of the county could not carry him to many of the schools which were spread across 3,000 square miles.

In the same year that Mr. Schroeder was advertising the teaching of German, Inspector Scott was grumbling in his annual reports about the irregularity of attendance. He wrote in 1888, "It must be remembered that in rural sections there are two sets of pupils, one of which can attend only in the fall and winter months, and the other from spring to fall." The average daily attendance in the rural schools was 43 per cent of the number enrolled. The inspector speculated, " I have no doubt an improvement in the course of studies prescribed for public schools, whereby subjects of more practical utility were substituted for many of those now taught, would effect a

85

great improvement in the regularity of attendance as could possibly be obtained." He made this comment in the same year, 1888, that elementary education was reported to be general and compulsory throughout Germany. Some proof of its efficacy was the claim that only 1.06 per cent of the recruits in the army in that country could neither read nor write.

Inspector Scott's prophecy was fulfilled about 25 years later. In some rural townships, such as Wilberforce, there were some school sections where all the pupils came from German families, and the German language prevailed to such an extent that education was threatened. A ruling of the provincial department of education in 1890 had made English the obligatory language of elementary school instruction, but at S.S. #8 Wilberforce Township, a school section named Germanicus, the pupils attended less than half the time. North Renfrew's Inspector in 1912, E.T. White, found that classes at this one-roomed brick school, built in 1909 on land purchased from William Wolfgram, were disorganised by the absence of the 70 children who attended 'German schools' elsewhere on Mondays, Tuesdays and Wednesdays. Such behavior was an obstacle to any progress in the reading and writing of English, but a school teacher of that year, a Miss Isabel V. Guenther, devised a solution to the problem, which met the inspector's approval.

Realizing that many of the subjects taught at Public Schools had little appeal for pupils who lived in the country, she introduced agriculture into the curriculum. Miss Guenther supplemented theory by encouraging the children to plant and care for a garden on the school grounds; it was a venture that succeeded beyond her expectations. So devoted did her pupils become to their crops of vegetables that they refused to allow anyone else to care for them during the summer vacation. A faded newspaper of 1913 shows a 1912 photograph of girls in ankle-length dresses industriously hoeing around cabbages while the boys pose proudly beside tall stalks of corn. Having first established her students' interest in agriculture and nature study, Miss Guenther furnished the school's library that fall with appropriate books, such as King's "Soils", James' "Agriculture" and Hodge's "Nature Study and Life". For the first time the children in her classes began to read in English without reluctance.

The teacher's ingenuity was commended by the school inspector who reported: "The progress made at the school in agricultural education was remarkable... and the results were no less noticeable in other ways such as, for instance, in the matter of writing compositions." In this respect, the children had been deficient because they were of German extraction, according to the inspector, but on his last visit he had found them more proficient in composition than the average child of English-speaking parents.

Although the one-roomed school at Germanicus and the one-roomed school at nearby Budd Mills were filled to overflowing with pupils in the years before the first world war, the potential for agriculture in this part of Ontario was no longer advertised by governments. The western provinces of Canada beckoned to immigrants from Europe who crossed the Atlantic in search of land and opportunity. Even within the established farming families in Renfrew Coiunty, the attractions of an easier life elsewhere were well known. In large families, some sons would have to move away, out of the county, if they wanted farms of their own. Discussion of the merits of faming in other parts of Canada reached the pages of the Deutsche Post, the weekly newspaper in the German language which was published in Arnprior first in 1901 and then in Pembroke from 1906 to 1916. Its contents included local news from 'stringers' throughout eastern Ontario, although much of its space was devoted to syndicated foreign news, especially from Germany.

MOST WERE ABSENT ON MONDAYS AND TUESDAYS
At S.S. No. 7 Alice Township, most of the pupils at this public school in Locksley in 1903 were from German families. According to William Stresman, who was too young to attend school when this photograph was taken, the German children went to a 'German school' on Monday and Tuesday mornings; there they were taught by the pastor of the local Lutheran church in the German language.
Mr. Stresman, born 1898, could identify all the pupils except one.
Top row, left to right: Sam Radtke, George McCauley, Ray Graham, Alex Bucholtz, Martha Biesenthal, the teacher Miss Minnie Cobourn.
Second row: Annie Stresman, Minnie Bucholtz, Della Biesenthal, Cassie Biggs, Adolph Biesenthal, Frank Risto, Henry Hass, Struthers Montgomery, Ferdinand Biesenthal and Dora Mau.
Bottom row: Gertie and Dora Bucholtz, Emma Radtke, Sam Hass, Clara Biesenthal, Florence Frivalt, Ernest Risto, Stanley Graham, Herman Mau and one unknown girl.
Photograph by Rev. Louis D. Zimmerman, pastor 1896-1907 of Grace Lutheran Church, Locksley, Alice Township.

TEACHER FACED DISCRIMINATION

Miss Elsie Wienke (standing at the door flanked by two school trustees) was only 19 years old when she taught 70 pupils from German families at this public school in Budd Mills, a hamlet in Renfrew County, in 1913. Her capable handling of so many children in one room is still remembered by senior citizens in this area of Wilberforce Township which was settled exclusively by German immigrants. Despite the teacher's abilities, she encountered prejudice when she applied for a promotion in 1919, because the Renfrew County Board of Education was alarmed by her German surname.

Photograph reproduced courtesy Wesley Budd, Budd Mills.

NO LONGER A LANGUAGE BARRIER AT GERMANICUS

The school at Germanicus, S.S. No. 8 Wilberforce Township, was acclaimed as a "model school" in 1912 by North Renfrew's Public School Inspector E.T. White because of the teacher's success in persuading her 70 German-speaking pupils to read English. The last teacher there in 1968, Mrs. James Miller, had 29 pupils, some with German names but none who could speak the German language fluently. Hanging on the fence are: Lorraine Kaija, Carol Schauer, Rhonda McDonald, Donna Brose, Glenda Lang, Wendy Wieland, Roy Zohr, Roy Raeder, Anthony Kaija, Glen Keuhl, Phyllis Borutski, Lois Kutschke, Ronnie Borutski, Grant Schauer, Leonard Blank, Lennox Sterling, Ronnie LaRose, Kenny Schauer, David Liedtke, Donnie Millark, Donna Borutski, Audrey Liedtke, Leanne Thur, Karen Sterling, Steven McDonald, Brenda Wieland and Doreen Blank.
Absent were Teresa Jeffrey and Myles Klingbeil.
The pupils, with origins as diverse as Finland, Scotland, Poland and Germany, all spoke English.

TWO RURAL SCHOOL SECTIONS UNITED
in 1925, IN AUGSBURG

"A fine one-roomed structure entirely creditable to the section," commented South Renfrew's Public School Inspector, G.G. McNab in his annual report for 1925. Completed that year, this building of concrete block at Augsburg was designed to serve the pupils of S.S. No. 3 and S.S. No. 5 Grattan Township, which had united. The issue of rural school consolidation had been raised by Inspector McNab as early as 1919, but it was not fully accommodated until 1968. In its last year as a school, this building accommodated only Grades 5 to 8, the junior grades of the area being taught at another one-roomed school. In the winter months a skating-rink beside the school provided exercise during recess and a respite for the teacher, Mrs. Ormal Schroeder, from her 24 pupils.

On opposite page:

OLD SCHOOL PUMP

A birch tree now grows through the rotting wooden well cover and envelops the iron pump that once served S.S. #8 Raglan Township; the school building glimpsed through the leafless branches was the second on this site and was closed in 1952. The school, the church and the burial ground of a pioneer community were commonly located on the same piece of ground. At this location, near Palmer Rapids, only the burial ground remains in use. The iron pump still draws water and is occasionally employed in the watering of plants, hence the recent attachment to the arm.

AUCTION SALE
—OF—
Farm Property
At Mud Lake, Township of
South Algona

Wed'y, December 13, 1922
At. 2 o'clock, p.m.

Under instructions from the undersigned owner, I will offer for sale by Public Auction, subject to a reserve bid, 100 acres of good farm land at Mud Lake, township of South Algona, composed of half of lot 2 and half of 3 in concession 5. 60 acres under cultivation, balance in bush and timber. The soil is a heavy hardwood loam. Fair buildings—dwelling house, barn, stables, etc. On the premises are 3 or 4 carloads of peeled poplar pulpwood, one carload ready for market which is contracted with Mr. L. George at Eganville.

Abundant water supply from never-failing spring and well.

A quarter mile distant is Augsburg, where is located a German church, also a German school, an English school and a store and blacksmith shop.

An opportunity to purchase a valuable property, conveniently situated, at a moderate price. Sale will be conducted on owner's property.

Terms and conditions made known on day of sale.

JULIUS. J. SCHAUER,   GEO REEVES,
Owner,   Auctioneer.
R.R. 5, Eganville.

AUGSBURG HAD A GERMAN SCHOOL IN 1922

According to the 50th Anniversary Booklet of the Canada Synod of the Lutheran Church in Canada, published in 1911, there were no German parochial schools in the synod by that time. There were 44 schools where pastors provided religious instruction on Saturdays or weekdays, in addition to 66 Sunday schools. Truancy, caused by children attending German schools on weekdays, was a recurring problem in the rural townships until the 1930s, judging from the annual reports of the public school inspectors of Renfrew County.

Advertisement reproduced courtesy The Eganville Leader.

LETTERKENNY SCHOOL WITH 8 GRADES AND 25 PUPILS
At S.S. No. 4 Brudenell and Lyndoch Townships, the frame building of the 19th century school had been covered with siding of imitation brick. One of the schools that must have been visited by Inspector R.G. Scott, this one had been supplied by hydro power in later years, but wood was still used to heat the classroom and there was no indoor plumbing. A school bus brought children from a radius of about five miles to this one-roomed structure where the teacher, Mrs. Jean Hartwick, taught Grades one to eight to her 25 pupils, all of them from German families. In his annual report of 1926, South Renfrew's Public School Inspector G.G. McNab described some of the disadvantages of the small school: "Healthy rivalry so essential as an incentive to better work is lacking and so the progress of the pupil is impaired. Organized play is out of the question and so the play instinct, so valuable to the child, cannot find adequate expression..."
When this school closed in 1968 the pupils were admitted to a larger elementary school at Palmer Rapids.

On January 28, 1913, a man who was visiting relatives on a farm in Germanicus, Wilberforce Township, wrote a letter to the editor of the Deutsche Post, in which he belittled the opportunities of farming life in eastern Ontario. This man had settled in Maple Creek, Saskatchewan, in May 1911, and there had acquired "one quarter section homesteading and one quarter section pre-emption, total 320 acres". This, he claimed, was clean prairie land and especially good for growing wheat. The western farmer asserted that there was very little snow in Saskatchewan and the cattle could stay on pasture all year, eating the prairie grass which was just as succulent in the winter as in the summer. He concluded a long list of prices for produce by declaring, "It is not nearly so hard to be a farmer in Saskatchewan as in Ontario, because on the prairie you sow and harvest a crop the first year. The first year you sow flax and after that wheat year after year. The settling of Maple Creek is just a few years old, and it is too bad that not more farmers from Ontario move out there."

Excursions by train to Manitoba for farm laborers in the fall cost as little as $12 for a one-way ticket in 1905, but some of the German immigrants in Renfrew County were beginning to consider another agricultural frontier in northern Ontario that year. In Germanicus, Wilberforce Township, where the 1901 census shows that the area was densely settled by German people at that time, a 59-year-old blacksmith and farmer, August Kruger, set forth in early 1905 to explore the land beyond the railway terminus at New Liskeard. He had two sons from his first marriage, Bill and Joseph, and five more sons from his second marriage, Frank, Adolph, Ernest, Albert and Paul, as well as a daughter, Mary. August Kruger must have realised that not all his sons could expect to own a farm close to home, though he himself had been able to purchase three lots in Germanicus from an earlier German settler, William Berger. It was from this, that the father and one son, Frank, began their journey. The Temiskaming and Northern Ontario Railways had started construction out of North Bay in the summer of 1901 and had got as far as New Liskeard in January 1905. The two Krugers travelled by train as far as the tracks were laid, and then continued by boat to Tomstown on the Blanche River and on foot to Englehart. There they

HARVEST EXCURSIONS WERE CHEAP IN 1905
Cheap fares on the harvester trains enabled the men of eastern Ontario to visit the farmlands of the western provinces without committing themselves. Many went on these trips to earn extra money and have an adventure, but some would be tempted to return. As early as 1872 the Free Land Homestead Act had allowed the newcomer to the prairies to occupy a quarter-section of land (160 acres); if he met his obligations in improving it within a certain time limit, he could pre-empt a second quarter-section nearby for a nominal sum. Advertisements such as these were published until the 1920s in the weekly newspaper that circulated in the western townships of Renfrew County.

```
The Eganville Leader.
     Aug. 11, 1905.
```

Farm Laborers' Excursions.

Sept. 16th, 1905.—From all stations in Ontario, Sault Ste. Marie, Sudbury, Marberley and East, and Stations east of Kingston.

Tickets will be sold to female as well as to male laborers, but will not be sold at half rate to children.

At Winnipeg the special trains will be met by farmers and by representatives of the Manitoba Government. Laborers may engage with them at Winnipeg, and ticket agent will issue free ticket from Winnipeg to C. P. R. station where he has engaged to work.

After a laborer has worked for at least thirty days, and has certificate signed by the farmer with whom he has worked, such certificate will be honored prior to Nov. 30th for a ticket to return to starting point by same route as on going journey, on payment of $18.00.

150 lbs. baggage, wearing apparel only, will be allowed on each ticket, and each piece of baggage checked should bear the name of the owner, and show their home address. It will be readily understood that some difficulty may be experienced in handling some thousands of pieces of baggage at one station. Therefore, when possible, baggage should be carried in hand grips, which passengers should take in the cars with them.

Further information will be supplied on application to any Canadian Pacific Railway ticket agent. Intending excursionists should notify nearest ticket agent at once. See advertisement in this column.

WOOL WANTED.

At Eganville Woollen Mills. 27c. trade or 28c. cash per lb.—JNO. CHILDERHOSE & SONS.

Farm Laborers'
EXCURSIONS
2nd CLASS
To Manitoba and Assinaboia
$12.00

Sept. 16th, From stations in Ontario, Soo Ste. Marie, Ont., Sudbury, Maberley and east, and Stations east of Kingston.

One way tickets to Winnipeg only will be sold, with a certificate extending the trip before Sept. 15th, without additional cost, to given points in Manitoba and Assinaboia, if purchasers engage as farm laborers at Winnipeg, provided such farm laborers will work not less than 30 days at harvesting, and produce certificate to that effect, they will be returned to original starting point at $18.00, on or before November 30th, 1905. For further particulars apply to nearest Canadian Pacific Railway Ticket Agent.

C. WHITE, Agent,
Eganville, Ont.

KRUGER HOME IN RENFREW COUNTY

This one-and-a-half storey log farmhouse was the home of the family of August Kruger in Germanicus, Wilberforce Township, until 1905, the year that they moved to northern Ontario in search of new lands to conquer. The identity of the builder of this log house is not known; the property was purchased by August Kruger from a Free Grant settler in 1879. This building, with some modifications was still occupied in 1986, the inhabitants being Mr. and Mrs. Wilfred Miller who found there documents of the earlier owners.

BARN-RAISING. c. 1912. AT KRUGERDORF

Raised in Renfrew County, these sons of German immigrants, the Richters, the Kants, the Digullas and the Krugers, combined their efforts to build a barn on the farm of Mrs. August Kruger, who had been widowed in 1908. By that time sawn timber was commonly used on farms in Renfrew County because a number of steam-powered sawmills had been established. The construction of a barn from sawn timber demanded a different technique to that used in the earlier barns made of squared logs.

In this barn being built at Krugersdorf, the sills and horizontal members have been mortised into the principal posts and diagonal bracings attach these posts laterally to the second floor beams. The entrance, wide enough for a team of horses, will be on the long side, not the gable end. The two women, believed to be Mrs. Kruger and her daughter, would have to prepare a substantial quantity of food for the 27 workers.

Photograph reproduced courtesy Mrs. Alma Allsop, Kirkland Lake.

found that the lots were already taken, so they proceeded farther into the bush. The land they found in Chamberlain Township lay within an area of the Temiskaming valley known as the Little Clay Belt, and here the public lands had been surveyed and opened for settlement at the price of 50 cents per acre, subject to certain conditions. Residence of four years on the land, construction of a house at least 16 feet by 20 feet and the cultivation of a minimum of 10 acres out of every 100 acres were the requirements of the settlers. Mr. Kruger and his son built a small house and a blacksmith shop before sending for the rest of the family, and sold two of their three lots in Renfrew County for $975 in May 1905. The decision had been made to stay.

At first, August Kruger worked as a blacksmith for the railway, making spikes and shoeing horses but the land must have proved fertile for The Deutsche Post on February 7, 1907, reported that this German pioneer had acquired 820 acres of land near New Liskeard "where he and his sons are building a new homestead". When the Temiskaming and Northern Ontario Railway laid tracks through the township of Chamberlain in 1906, the rail lines passed close to one of the Kruger homesteads. It was not surprising that others from the Germanicus-Golden Lake-Augsburg area of Renfrew County made the trip to have a look at the promising new countryside.

One visitor in 1906 was Otto Kant, one of the younger sons of an emigrant from West Prussia who had settled in South Algona in 1871. Otto returned to his brothers with tales of "milk and honey". The land where the Krugers had settled was free from stone (incredible news to anyone who had farmed in the western townships of Renfrew County). The ground in Chamberlain Township was level and well-watered on three sides by the Aidie Creek and the winding Blanche River. It was by now easily accessible by a railway that ran through 70 miles of wilderness, north of North Bay, before it reached the shores of Lake Temiskaming. Those who chose to pioneer in northern Ontario could take their household furnishings, farming equipment and livestock, an advantage that European immigrants had not known when they crossed the Atlantic ocean.

Otto Kant moved to Krugerdorf in 1906 and because of his glowing accounts of life there two of his brothers, David and Edward, were persuaded to join him in later years, to uproot their families and try their fortunes in farming. From the railway station in Golden Lake one day in May 1910, there was a cavalcade of German families, the Kants, the Richters, and the Digullas, all leaving their first Canadian home for a second. The scene was a familiar one in Renfrew County; boxcars of Irish families's effects were accompanying the young and restless, also heading north or west.

The German families were travelling north to Krugerdorf, where they would join people who spoke the same language. Eight miles north of Englehart, where the railway crossed the Blanche River, the train stopped at a flag station and the boxcars were unloaded. The settlers' belongings were deposited beside the railway track and

AT KRUGERDORF
Construction of the "Kruger-house", c. 1918, which was being built by the Kruger sons for their widowed mother, Mrs. August Kruger, followed the style of the one-and-a-half storey house commonly found in Renfrew County, although it was made of sawn lumber, later covered by siding. It was still standing, though unoccupied, in 1979. Mrs. August Kruger lived here until 1944, when she moved back to Renfrew County at the age of 87, to live with her daughter, Mary.

had to be portaged in wagonloads to the new homes which would be located on lots of 160 acres. Lumber had been taken in order to build the first dwellings and barns, for there were no big pines to be felled and squared for use, as there had been in eastern Ontario. The first homes of the Krugers were merely tarpaper shacks, and when a daughter was born to Frank and Annie Kruger in 1909 the mother feared that the baby would freeze to death.

With no large stumps to uproot, and with a rich clay soil, the farms were soon cleared and planted. The crops grew well and barns were needed to hold the harvest of hay and grains. Sawn lumber was available, for the Kruger family had established a steam-powered sawmill beside the Blanche Riber. Steam power was also used to run the Krugers' threshing-mill, another boon to the farmers. The men earned extra money in wintertime by going away to work in the lumber camps, another tradition that had been experienced by their fathers in Renfrew County. In this community there was no need for home-made furniture or hand-made textiles. With the convenience of railway which could deliver goods from catalogues, the residents ordered what they needed. There was a general store at Krugerdorf, operated by Moses Vertlieb, which supplied small items such as salt, sugar, candy and soft drinks. Groceries that were bulky might be purchased at Englehart, although the earliest settlers had to walk a round trip of 16 miles, there and back, and carry their groceries home on their backs, before roads were made to allow the passage of horse-drawn vehicles.

There was no doctor in the community. The infant mortality rate was high and the need for a burial ground became urgent even before the construction of a church. David Kant sold a piece of his property for a church and cemetery, and burials were made there for several years before a building, Zion Lutheran Church of the Missouri Synod, was constructed in 1912, by the volunteer labour of the men of the congregation.

"Before that time we met for services either at the Krugers' home or at our house, or at any place that was big enough," recalled Ferdinand Eduard Otto Kant, the oldest son of David Kant, born in 1898. After the church was erected, a parsonage was built to accomodate a minister, for the congregation swelled and included members who came from Cobalt and Haileybury. The services were held in the German language, the everyday language spoken by the community, aided in its survival by the German catechism schools held by the pastor.

" I can remember reading my German catechism with one hand, churning the milk with the other and rocking

AT KRUGERDORF

At the general store in Krugerdorf, c. 1918, the three farmers enjoying refreshments include John Quast (left) who celebrated his 90th birthday in this community in 1980. The horse-drawn vehicle owned by Frank Kruger was being used to take his visiting in-laws on a trip around Krugerdorf; his father-in-law, bearded Fred Quast, sits in front and his wife behind him, with several daughters squeezed on to the seats of the 'Democrat'. One daughter, Anna, was Mrs. Frank Kruger. The Quasts came from Augsburg, near Eganville, and had travelled to Krugerdorf by train.

Photographs reproduced courtesy Ferdinand Kant, Iroquois Falls.

THRESHING WITH A STEAM ENGINE.
c. 1912. AT KRUGERDORF

Adolph Kruger, standing on the right, was one of the sons of August Kruger who attempted to establish a new agricultural and German-speaking community in Chamberlain Township in the Temiskaming region. In this scene men are threshing oats, using power supplied by a steam engine, and storing the grain which was used as a feed for horses.

Photograph reproduced courtesy Mrs. Alma Allsop (nee Kruger), Kirkland Lake.

the cradle with my feet," remembered Mr. Kant, who was fluent in German and nicknamed "Fern". An elementary school, conducted in English, had been organised for the children, but the young girl who was employed as a teacher had received less education than the Kant boy who therefore felt it was a waste of his time. His labours were considered necessary on the farm, as he discovered when he tried to enlist in the army during the First World War. His father successfuly opposed the attempt on the grounds that his son was needed at home.

Loyal to the country that their grandparents had chosen, there were other young men from Krugerdorf who left the farm in order to serve in the armed forces. One son of August Kruger's first marriage, William, had earlier chosen the army as his career and served with distinction in several wars, being awarded the Military Cross in 1918. Nevertheless, when the Second World War was in progress, a petition was sent to Queen's Park, Toronto, by residents of the Englehart district, which urged the provincial government to change the name of Krugerdorf to one of the following — Wavell, McNaughton, Battlewon, Bishop or Pioneer. By this time the rural community had dwindled in numbers and English-speaking immigrants from the Toronto area had long since diluted the German identity of the settlement, which now also contained a Jewish cemetery. Mrs. August Kruger was still living there and her youngest son, Paul, reacted violently to the petition.

Voicing his displeasure to the newspapers in February 1941, P.J. Kruger described himself as a son of the Renfrew County family whose members were the first permanent settlers in that area. After relating how his family had relocated in Chamberlain township about six months before the railway arrived, Mr. Kruger related, "When the railway commission of the day took over the line, it was considered appropriate that the station there should be named after the first permanent settler, and that the post office opened later, take the same name and not through any request of the Kruger family." The petition to change the name was unsuccessful.

(Krugersdorf was the name assigned to the post office, but the community is still labelled as Krugerdorf on large-scale maps such as Englehart 31M/13, published by the Surveys and Mapping Branch of the Department of Energy, Mines and Resources.)

Until 1924 the church at Krugerdorf had its own pastor, Reverend Walter Biesenthal, himself a native of Renfrew County. He left the parish in 1925, although the church that year had 174 souls in its congregation and a Sunday school with 23 pupils. In 1924 there had been seven baptisms and 17 confirmations, but pastoral duties in later years would consist largely of burials and services from a visiting minister, and services would no longer be held in the German language.

Many had left Krugerdorf to work in the mines of northern Ontario or on the railways. David Kant was one disillusioned farmer who sold his property after nine years of work, returning to work on the railway. Others followed his example. The short growing season and the lack of markets as the lumber camps moved farther away had made the agricultural enterprise unprofitable. The few that remained to farm the land have been growing feed crops and caring for dairy cattle, and the names on the mail-boxes, such as Quast and Digulla, show that a number of descendants of the pioneers are still living in the area.

Camp Petawawa

While the Krugers were travelling north to find new lands in Ontario where they could farm, another chapter of change in the settlement of Renfrew County by German immigrants was taking place in Petawawa Township. From 1885 to 1905 a community of farmers had taken up land in lots adjoining the Ottawa River and in a corridor of lots that extended 12 lots back from the river. They had built their own Lutheran church and organized School Section #4 Petawawa Township. Most of them were German-speaking immigrants or the sons of immigrants, although a sketch-map of the area at that time shows a few British names and at least one that was French. Chosen by the Department of Militia as a training camp for the army, this land was bought by an agent of the government, a Pembroke lawyer, who negotiated first with the farmers along the shoreline and later with those living inland. Some of the German farmers appear to have been willing to sell their properties in 1905, while others were still holding out in 1909, but the ultimate aim of the government — to establish a military training camp which had no civilians living within its boundaries — was eventually met. Canadian Forces Base, Camp Petawawa, now occupies 140 square miles, and all that remains of that early German presence if a small fenced cemetery of St. Matthew's Lutheran Church. Since the cemetery is contained in the area where firing practice is held, it is difficult for the public to visit there.

This military base in Petawawa township became the scene of an internment camp for aliens during the First World War, and it undoubtedly contributed to the irritation and anti-German prejudices that began to surface in Pembroke in 1915. An Order-in-Council of October 28, 1914, authorized civilian registrars to detain suspected aliens in camps for the duration of hostilities, making it clear that internees were prisoners of war, not convicts. In a country of scarcely more than seven million people, 393,320 told the 1911 census-takers that they were of German origin.

Major-General Sir William Otter, 69, was summoned out of retirement to command the internment operations, and on Nov. 1, 1914, he was made responsible for the accomodation, feeding, maintenance and employment of the internees, who would be supervised by guards from the Militia Department. Buildings across the land were hastily requisitioned to house these men, and Otter argued for a work camp at Petawawa, where roads and land clearance might usefully expand the country's largest military camp. This site had been the

THE ARMY ARRIVES IN PETAWAWA TOWNSHIP
In August 1905 government spokesmen announced that the R.C.F.A. would be encamped at Petawawa for firing practice that summer. All 24 field batteries in Canada would take part. There were no permanent buildings that first summer and the men lived in tents. The families of German farmers had to be moved off their properties on a daily basis when firing began, and since they showed resistance to this plan the settlers had to be 'bought out'.
Photograph reproduced courtesy Darlene Gunter, Pembroke.

WARTIME INTERNMENT OF GERMAN PEOPLE AT PETAWAWA
In the winter of 1915, Canadian guards lead and escort lines of marching German 'aliens' imprisoned at an internment camp at Petawawa. The presence of this camp, nine miles west of Pembroke, aggravated suspicions that fires and explosions at munitions plants in Renfrew County might be due to sabotage.
Photograph reproduced courtesy Mrs. Manse Haley, Smiths Falls.

scene of the largest mobilization in the history of Canada in June, 1914, with at least 12,000 cavalary, infantry and artillery accomodated on the grounds. Otter's request was granted and the vacated buildings at Petawawa's military base became the first internment camp to be chosen. It was not the most tactful choice, but the general was probably unaware that the land had originally been acquired, cleared, cultivated by and expropriated from, German immigrants.

By January 28, 1915, the 1,000 internees at Camp Petawawa were the subject of comment in the local press. A mixture of Austrians, who were Roman Catholics, and Germans, who were Lutherans, they were reported to be employed at cutting roads and felling trees. Visiting pastors from the Lutheran churches were able to minister to the German internees in the German tongue, for that was still the customary language used in the homes and churches of Pembroke, Petawawa and the north-western townships of Renfrew County where the rural population was predominantly German in origin.

The first hint of trouble at the Petawawa internment camp was reported in July, 1915, when 500 prisoners refused to work and were placed on a bread and water diet. There were some escapes that summer, but an armed posse captured the escaped men within a few miles of the camp. More serious alarm was caused in September, when prisoners escaped and were not caught; the countryside for miles around was occupied by farms owned by people of German descent. Another strike of the interned men occurred when the authorities tried to compel them to work on a religous day. While all these altercations at the camp were being reported in The Pembroke Observer and The Pembroke Standard, the newspapers were also featuring accounts of patriotic meetings, which included the collection of funds to aid the fight in Europe. There were even poems, presumably

Occupants of land in Petawawa Township, in the area where the federal government began to acquire property and to establish a military camp in 1905 as shown by the Assessment Rolls completed April 10, 1905, & land records

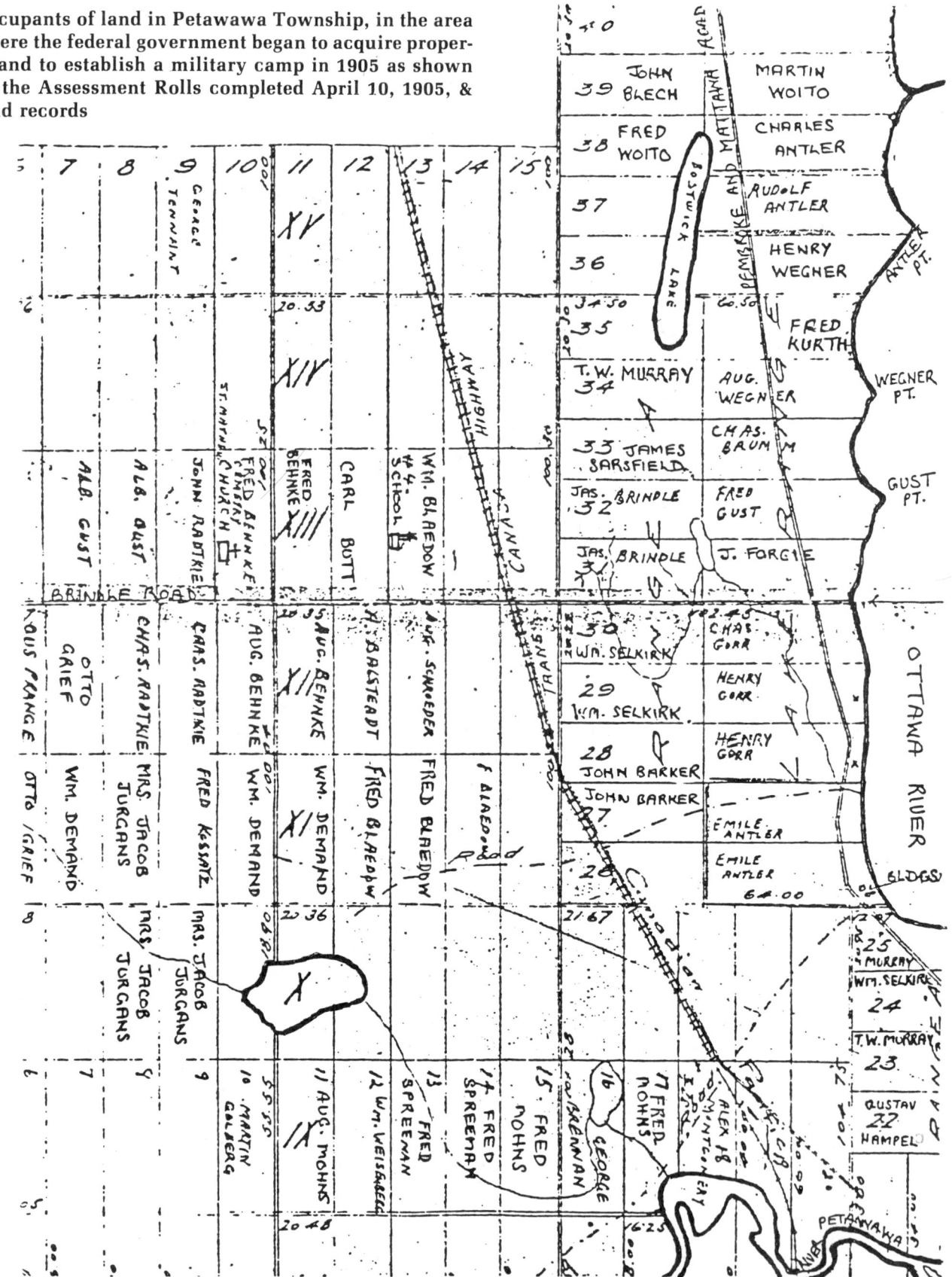

by local poets, which bemoaned the downfall and moral values in Germany.

The English weekly newspapers in Pembroke and the one in Eganville had at first refrained from expressing controversial opinions, in fact the care with which they disassociated themselves from the news stories that they reproduced from other sources suggests that they were eager to avoid losing readers of German descent. This cautious neutrality was breached at the end of 1915.

The Pembroke Observer was the first to disclose, in its issue of December 2, the uneasiness that had been felt by some residents. "Quite a sensation has been caused in Pembroke this week by the publication in The Ottawa Journal on Tuesday of a lengthy interview given by Mayor Morris and which casts suspicion on many of our German residents, and alleges that the town is the centre of an organized spy system, the machinations of which are being carried all over Canada... It is a fact known to all that some residents German extraction have at times since the outbreak of war given expression to sentiments and opinions of a nature calculated to arouse the antipathy of loyal citizens whose patriotism is stirred now as it has never been stirred before, and which, if made in Germany under similar circumstances by any one of British extraction, would probably merit for the person guilty a volley from a military firing squad. There has at times been much indignation caused by such indiscretions on the part of the people with the Teutonic cause, and no action has been taken to intern or in any way punish those who are believed to be openly unfriendly to the Empire, and this fact is as gall and wormwood not only to the Mayor but to many others whose anxiety for the Empire's cause is deep and sincere."

Though The Observer found it difficult to believe the charge that Pembroke was the centre of a spy system that embraced the whole country, it nevertheless reported the story. The paper assured its readers that its circulation area contained little that could be of any military value to the German authorities and declared that the prisoners interned at the Petawawa military camp were being decently treated. The issue of Dec. 2, 1915, did, however, contain a statement that might be interpreted as a warning.

"We are not going to indulge in any washy sentimentality regarding our fellow German citizens. We fancy they are intelligent enough to understand that no one would wish to do any injustice to people who have for so long a time had a large and important part in the business and social life of Pembroke and district, but if any among them assume an attitude hostile to the country at this time they should be dealt with as alien enemies and the authorities should have no hesitation in invoking the law, quite irrespective of any political or other considerations."

Such prominence was given to the stories emanating from out-of-town papers that the mayor J.L. Morris, felt obliged to write a letter to The Observer, giving his own version of the interview in The Ottawa Journal that had created such a furore. Having been asked point-blank whether there were any German spies in Pembroke, His Worship had replied, "Judging from the number of German spies in Europe and the United States, I think it would be reasonable to suppose that there might be a thousand in Canada, and from the proximity of Petawawa camp it would be expected that there might be some here." It was the mayor's opinion that the Ottawa paper had distorted his words in order to boost its circulation.

There were plants in Pembroke and in the town of Renfrew, 40 miles away, which were manufacturing munitions during this war. When two men of German background, from the Kitchener area, were discovered at the Pink works in Pembroke under suspicion of planning to wreck a munitions plant, they were fired on by the guards and subsequently arrested. (The Pink works had previously been a plant that manufactured tools for the logging industry.) The appearance of these men in court in Pembroke was reported on the front page of The Eganville Leader, March 17, 1916, in the same issue as an account of a fire which totally destroyed a shell factory in Renfrew. The cause of the fire was never determined, but innuendo continued in the local press.

Confinement of German nationals at the internment camp at Petawawa was ended soon after these occurrences. The Canadian guards were having trouble controlling their charges. When in May 1916 the situation assumed threatening proportions and appeared to become too serious for the Petawawa authorities to cope with, six carloads of 300 Austrians were transferred to Kapuskasing's internment camp in northern Ontario. When the new arrivals were ordered to do some camp chores they objectd to manual labour; so hostile were the attitudes and so serious the attempts to escape that the Canadian soldiers were compelled to fix bayonets in order to restrain the internees within the barbed wire enclosure, inflicting some wounds in the process. This contretemps was also reported in the English papers of Renfrew County.

The wounds inflicted by the treatment of people with German surnames and people of German descent would take longer to heal. The Pembroke War Memorial bears testimony to the fact that sons and grandsons of German immigrants to the Pembroke area had given their lives while fighting on the side of the British Empire in the 1914-1918 years. Yet the ownership of a German surname threatened to blight the career of residents who were third-generation Canadians. One small incident that was related in the press involved a young woman, Miss Elsie Wienke, a granddaugther of Wilhelm and Charlotte Wienke who had arrived in Canada in 1864. When she was only 19 years old, Miss Wienke was in charge of a one-roomed school at Budd Mills, which held 70 pupils in 1913. Six years after she taught in that German community in Wilberforce Township, this teacher was seeking promotion but found that her surname placed her at a disadvantage.

Local newspapers told their readers that Miss Wienke, whose relatives lived in the German settlement near Pembroke, had been appointed by the County Board of Education as an assistant in the kindergarten department of Hester Howe School despite the board's alarm over her German-sounding name. At one meeting, a Dr. Caroline Brown, described as a leading woman member of the board, had vigorously taken up the cudgels in favour of Miss Wienke. "She is a natural born Canadian," Dr. Brown is said to have commented, adding that Miss Wienke's two brothers had served gallantly overseas during the war, one of them earning the D.C.M.

HARVEST EXCURSIONS WERE STILL ATTRACTING FARM LABOR IN 1924

Cheap fares on the "harvester" trains enabled the men of eastern Canada to visit the farmlands of the western provinces without committing themselves. Many went on these trips to earn extra money and have a little adventure, but some would be tempted to remain permanently for the land was flat and free from stones. As early as 1872 the Free Land Homestead Act had allowed the newcomer to the prairies to occupy a quarter-section of land (160 acres); if he met his obligations in improving it within a certain time limit, he could 'pre-empt' a second quarter-section nearby for a nominal sum. (This advertisement was published in The Eganville Leader, August 22, 1924.)

Advertisement. The Eganville Leader. March 26, 1920.

"I WENT ON IT VERY POOR FIVE YEARS AGO". This advertisement, probably written by the farmer himself, provides a good description of a 200-acre farm in Renfrew County in 1920. Despite its apparent success, William A. Radtke moved south of the border and in July of that year he was writing letters to the editor of The Eganville Leader, in praise of the superior farming land of New York State.

Auction Sale
Farm, Live Stock and Implements

Under instructions from the undersigned owner, I will offer for sale by Public Auction at his premises—Lots 11 and 12, Concession 3, of the

Township of South Algona

About three miles distant from Mud Lake Corners, on

Monday, April 10th, 1922

Beginning at 12.30 o'clock, p.m., the following:
1 mare, five-year-old
1 colt, a year old in June
Cattle and sheep
Set American harness
Set coarse-fine single harness
Set fine single harness and collars
Set working harness
Set driving harness—good as new
Bridles and halters
1 cutter, 2 double buggies
3 single buggies, 1 iron truck wagon
Light wagon, cart, wheelbarrow
2 mowers—Deering and Massey-Harris
Moody binder, Massey-Harris binder
1 frame sleigh, pair sloops
1 seed sower, wooden roller, cultivator
2 walking plows, 2 springtooth harrows
Yankee plow—Frost and Wood
1 finishing harrow, pair wire stretchers
1 crosscut saw, 3 hand saws
Sawing arbor, wringer and stand
Box stove, cook stove, heating stove
Grain cradle, scythes and snaths, cooler
10 bags peas, 2 wooden beds
Grindstone, 3 cupboards, big barrel
Table, lantern, muzzle-loading gun
Sheep shears, horse bells, lash whip
Neckyokes, whiffletrees, hayfork
Trough, wagon axle and tongue—
Clippers, bench axe, shovels, brace, bits and augers, planes, steel square, forks, wrenches, drawknife, plow handles, house doors, window sashes, grain hasher and bagger, 2 strawcutters and many other small articles found about a farm

TERMS:—$10 and under, cash; over that amount 6 months' credit on a joint note at 6 per cent.

There will also be offered for sale, farm of 150 acres. 50 acres under cultivation, 50 acres pasture and 50 acres bush. On the premises are a dwelling house with kitchen, horse stable and sheep stable, granary, shed and barn, pig house and hen house. A splendid well provides a never failing supply of good water.

Everybody invited to this Big Sale.

FRANK J. SCHRUDER,
Owner, Eganville—R.R. 2.
THOS. F. BURGESS,
Auctioneer, Cobden.

AWAY TO THE ANTIQUE STORES

On Saturday, June 2, 1979, an auction sale was held at a farm in South Algona Township, where the grandson of a German immigrant had decided to retire and sell the property. Edward Zadow who had settled here in 1881 was the brother of a trained furniture-maker, J. Albert Zadow, whose initials appeared on the back of one of the pine cupboards.

A visiting picker outbid local competitors and loaded his truck with the clothes cupboard, the kitchen cupboard, the wool-winder, the dough-box, the benches and even the firewood box that had been used by three generations of Zadows.

GERMAN CUPBOARD AT AN ANTIQUE SHOW

At an antique show in 1980, this cupboard was labelled "German cupboard from Renfrew County. $2,200". It had no further clues to its identity. The style of this pine cupboard, with its deep pie shelf and scalloped top, was typical of some of the German furniture-makers in Renfrew County, but its origin would be known only to the picker or dealer who bought it from its first home.

This pew came from the Evangelical church on the Marsh Road in Wilberforce Township, near Rankin. This brick church was closed in 1967 when the congregation had declined to two families, a total of ten members, and the building (constructed in 1907) has been made into a home.

The feelings of resentment about treatment during and after those war years are still alive in the memories of German families in the Pembroke area, although few members are old enough to have experienced them first hand. Conversely, the suspicions harboured by those who believed that those who were of German descent supported the country that the British Commonwealth forces were fighting are still being voiced, generally by senior citizens. In actual fact, not one charge of sabotage or espionage or sedition was ever proved, but there are plenty of people living in the county who will argue about it.

The fact that a large number of small farms that changed hands soon after the war ended seems to have been prompted by a desire to try new pastures rather than any wish to escape the climate of hostility in Renfrew County. The advertisements are revealing.

In 1922, the advertisements included harnesses, cutters and buggies, which would be useful items for anyone living in the rural townships where roads were poor and the automobile unknown. A Forest Beauty cookstove was a practical item for the housewife, not the valuable collectible it now is. The washstands, the wardrobes, the bread-box (the dough-box), the cupboards, the looms, the rocking-chairs, even the chaff fork, were sold at auction sales for use on other farms in 1922, but now they have a value that would astonish the people who made them and the people who once used them.

At the site of the first Lutheran church in the Ottawa Valley, on a corner lot on the B-Line in Alice Township, there is now just a clearing and a plaque on a boulder; nearby on a sloping ground may be found the remains of the cemetery of St. Paul's Lutheran Church founded by Rev. L.H. Gerndt in 1862. Many other churches in the rural townships have been demolished or closed down or converted into homes. The sight of church pews on farmhouse verandahs or in back yards is revealing evidence of the dwindling membership in some country congregations, which used to support a German-language church.

The drive sheds, which once sheltered horse-drawn transport while their owners attended church, are now scarce. The vehicles that were harnessed to horses are numerous and unwanted; the buggies and cutters still make an appearance at auction sales, and wagons can be

DOUGH-BOX ON BROADLOOM
The dough-box used to be kept in the kitchen where the heat from the wood stove helped the raising of the dough. Those who recall its use also remember the smell of stale yeast that clung to the dough-box no matter how well it was cleaned out, but times have changed. Rescued from an ignoble fate (it was headed for a township dump), this pine dough-box now rests on broadloom in someone's living-room; having been stripped of its paint, the dough-box shows the scars of a lifetime of use. The box has the usual sloping sides and is mounted on trestle ends which have an S-shape typical of German woodworkers. It came from a German farm in the Augsburg area.

PEWS GIVEN AWAY

As the congregations of the country churches diminished in numbers, the members have been obliged to accept the closing of these buildings. Improved roads have made it practical for them to journey to services farther away by car. The brick churches may be converted into homes, while the log churches are demolished and sold for the squared timbers. The pews, which are generally believed to date from the founding of the church, are distributed among the remaining members of the congregation; they are now seen on verandahs and lawns where they serve as benches with hard seats and straight backs. This pew came from the Zion Lutheran church in South Algona Township which was built in 1895 and removed in 1977.

TWO GERMAN CHURCHES, CLOSE AND SEPARATE

In Raglan Township, in the south-west corner of Renfrew County, St. Stephen's Lutheran church, Canada Synod, with its tall steeple is situated directly opposite the Emmanuel Evangelical United Church on the same road in the rural community of Schutt. Both congregations were founded in the 19th century when German immigrants were pioneering in this hilly bush countryside.

When the Evangelical church was destroyed by fire, May 18, 1977, its 75-member congregation was offered temporary accommodation for services in the Lutheran church. A new church costing $100,000 was constructed in six months on the same site. The Lutheran church was invited to take part in the services of dedication at the Evangelical church, October 30, 1977, all of them conducted in English.

SITE OF FIRST LUTHERAN CHURCH
At Locksley, Alice Township, St. Paul's Lutheran church was constructed in 1862 and burned down in 1882. The only visible gravestone is that of Johann Carl Demant, 1844-1905. The church site was commemorated in 1980; the ground was cleared and identified by a plaque attached to a boulder, a large stone from the Canadian Shield moved from a nearby construction site.

THE DRIVE SHED
This drive shed, beside St. John's Lutheran church (of the Missouri Synod) Germanicus, Wilberforce Township, could accommodate ten horse-drawn vehicles. Its age is unknown. When Johann Lipke retired from farming in 1912, he transferred his farm to his 42-year-old son, August, on condition that the father and his wife would be maintained in their accustomed comforts and life-style. One of the clauses in the 'maintenance mortgage' stipulated that the senior Lipkes and the survivor must be driven to this church every second Sunday, a distance of about a mile.

SILO ON A CENTURY FARM
The modern silo was erected October 17, 1978, on this Century Farm in Hagarty Township, initially settled by Matthew Noack from Brandenberg in 1862. The immigrant's first dwelling is the simple structure in front of the silo; the one-and-a-half storey log farmhouse was completed in 1905 and housed three generations of couples called Mr. and Mrs. Matthew Noack with their families. The third owner had daughters, but no sons, and the ownership of the farm was transferred to his grandson, also called Matthew, who continued to work the land.

On opposite page:

LETTERKENNY CHURCH, E.U.B. SIGN
The Evangelical Association began its work in Eastern Ontario in 1865 with a missionary, Rev. Peter Alles, who preached to scattered congregations in the German language. In 1880, a circuit rider, Rev. D.H. Brand, covered at route of 60 miles from Rockingham which included a congregation at Letterkenny, Brudenell Township. This church at Letterkenny was built in 1902. The Evangelical Association merged with the United Brethren, Nov. 16, 1946, and the churches subsequently bore the title of Evangelical United Brethren, as this sign shows.
A frame structure painted white with green trim, the Letterkenny church was rededicated in 1954, after many improvements, but it was closed in 1963. The only church in this hamlet, its membership had declined to 12.
The E.U.B. churches joined the United Church of Canada in 1968, thus the sign outside the Letterkenny church is obsolete in Canada.

found littering the fields. Blacksmiths have been replaced by service stations, and one of the German blacksmith's workshops from Renfrew County is now on display at the Ontario Agricultural Museum at Milton. The paved roads built in the 1930s have been a catalyst for change.

Signs that a farm is still a working farm may be measured by the appearance of upright silos that sprout beside log buildings constructed by the immigrants of the 19th century. More recent newcomers from Germany have changed the scenery by the way in which they make a living on the land. The wilderness setting has been used by some to provide tourist attractions and it is ironic that the isolation of untilled landscapes, rocky, forested and well-watered, now proves to be an asset for the owners.

A CENTURY FARM WITH A MODERN APPEARANCE
Born at Falkenstein, Kreis Studt, Frankfurt, Johann Frederick Ernst Saar emigrated to Canada in 1862 with his parents, who settled in Alice Township. Reaching the age of 18 years in 1867, the Saars' son bought a property from the Crown that year for the sum of $160, consisting of flat fertile land in Stafford Township close to the town of Pembroke. The fourth and fifth generations of this pioneer, Earl Saar and his sons, were farming this same soil (with increased acreage) a century later when the property earned its Century Farm plaque. Fire had destroyed the family's home in 1962 and the farm buildings that provided shelter and feed for a herd of dairy cattle were modern. Still pioneers, the Saars were the first family in Renfrew County to begin raising buffalo, with the purchase of three females in 1979.

CRUCIFIX AND CANDLESTICKS
Although the Chalk River woodcarver, Charles August Vollrath, avoided making models of people, he made an exception when he carved a crucifix for the altar of Trinity Lutheran church in Chalk River. This log church had been rescued from the German settlement on the Ottawa River waterfront of Petawawa Township in 1909, after the German farmers there had been persuaded to sell their properties to the Department of Militia. Moved to Chalk River, this Lutheran church was torn down in 1965 when the congregation joined the Lutheran church in Deep River. The crucifix and the pair of wooden candlesticks made by Vollrath are in the possession of one of Vollrath's daughters.

BOWLING BALLS
A reminder of simpler pleasures, these bowling balls made of solid maple were used at church picnics held by the congregation of St. John's Lutheran church, Germanicus (Missouri Synod). Newspaper advertisements from the 1920s urged parishioners to attend the annual picnic in Lubow's maple grow, close to the church. The bowling balls ended up at an antique dealer's store.

BLACKSMITH'S FORGE
On the farm of a German immigrant, Johann Gottlieb Lipke, at Germanicus, Wilberforce Township, a stone fireplace and chimney are all that remains of the blacksmith's workshop that was used by his oldest son, August, born in 1870. (It was built by another son, Frank.) August, who inherited the farm in 1912, not only performed the blacksmith's jobs that were needed on his own property, but also did all manner of ironwork for neighbours. His son, Eric, remembered that the blacksmith could make keys, tools, hinges and repairs to farm implements. As usual, the blacksmith's shed was built at a safe distance from the house because of the danger from fire.

BLACKSMITHS WERE NEEDED FOR HORSE-DRAWN TRANSPORT
Apprenticed to a blacksmith, William Pilatzke, in the years when horse-power meant horses, Barney Ristau (1897-1981) had learned to shoe a horse and make a rim for a wagon wheel, measured with a 'traveller'; the iron outer rim made in the forge was applied to the wooden wheel and cooled quickly so that it contracted and held the whole wheel together. In his workshop at Golden Lake the blacksmith kept a few horseshoes as a souvenir of the past, together with the 'traveller' that he made as an apprentice.

HORSE-DRAWN TRANSPORT
Buggies like this one were once the only method of speedy travel around Renfrew County; they were not replaced by the automobile until the 1930s. At auction sales on old German farms the horse-drawn transport of the first and second generation emerges from the barns, for sale to the highest bidder. This one was seen on the farm of Charles Runtz in Lyndoch Township, an immigrant who is mentioned in the 1881 census.

BLACKSMITH'S SHOP

The blacksmith's shop of Carl Potter on lot 32, con. nine, Brudenell Township, was located at the crossroads community of Rockingham. It had been closed for decades when this photograph (below) was taken in 1967, according to the owner of the property then, Ellis Kinder. In the 1871 census records, this blacksmith aged 33, and his wife Dorothee aged 24, were described as being German in origin, although the village of Rockingham was thoroughly English in character — it even had a cricket team. This building was purchased by a Toronto company and re-sold to the Ontario Agricultural Museum, Sept. 30, 1976. It was re-erected at Milton in 1977.

NEW SETTLERS FROM GERMANY IN RENFREW COUNTY

Among the newcomers who are settling on land in the western townships of Renfrew County are some recent immigrants from Germany, who are finding new ways to earn an income in a rural environment. (They are also building log houses in a different style from those of the pioneers.) Herbert Gerber, born 1906, forsook his nursery business in eastern Germany in 1956, and with his wife and five sons left the country; his married daughter and her husband escaped via Berlin and the family were reunited in Canada. After two years in Toronto, the Gerbers bought an old farm in South Algona Township where they established a nursery business. Improvement of the land included draining a swamp where Mr. Gerber is seen pruning young apple trees. Perennials, shrubs and trees grow out in the open, while a series of greenhouses shelter flowers for cutting and potted plants. Produce is trucked to florists in Ottawa and other centres in the Ottawa Valley. After 20 years of satisfying customers the Gerbers' Nursery is flourishing. The sons (for whose sake they emigrated) have all returned to live in Toronto, but the daughter and her family are carrying on the tradition.

WAGON

A four-wheeled vehicle for drawing heavy loads, the wagon was once an indispensible part of farm life. This one was made by Bill Luloff of Golden Lake (1859-1939), the village carpenter who could make anything from cradles to coffins. The hardware for his wagons was made by Gustave Hoch of Golden Lake (1862-1929), a blacksmith from Smotznern, Posen. A number of these wagons litter the ground around the abandoned sawmill at Budd Mills, which operated until 1963; the wagons were used to haul timber to the site.

Selected obituaries

In reading through the back copies of The Eganville Leader, up to and including 1939, I found firm evidence of the origin of the German pioneers in eastern Ontario. They were definitely born in Europe and not in southern Ontario, as some scholars have claimed. Their obituaries begin to appear in print shortly before the end of the first world war, for example, John Lisk, August 9, 1918. The lack of news about the German-born residents before this war, in an English language weekly such as The Leader, is probably explained by the popularity of a German language weekly in Renfrew County, the Deutsche Post, rather than by any prejudice. The Post was in print until the end of 1916, when it quietly folded at the behest of the editor.

These obituaries of pioneers have been selected arbitrarily, some because they had details that were of interest or because the people themselves were of significance. Peter Cutchaw who lived to be 103 and had 100 grandchildren was an obvious choice, as was Martin Budarick Jr., a member of the first German family to settle on land in Renfrew County, according to an 1860 report of an immigration agent. Bill Luloff of Golden Lake was a furniture-maker whose skill is now becoming appreciated, and the Pahls of Brudenell Township were pioneers whose lifetime of struggle is outlined in the obituary of the wife. Simon Chusroskie was the son of the father-and-son team who built the log farmhouse on view at the Champlain Trail Museum in Pembroke. Albert Kosmack was the postmaster at Vanbrugh for 48 years and William Michaelis was the first German immigrant to establish a business in Eganville.

The obituaries reflect the varying denominations of the German pioneers; they were Roman Catholic, Evangelical, Lutheran and even Presbyterian, the latter showing their readiness to adapt to life in a new country. The locations of the pioneers showed how they had spread through the townships of eastern Ontario. The lists of survivors show how the sons and daughters of the pioneers had scattered across North America, and how many had married sons and daughters of other German pioneers.

The following obituaries have been listed in alphabetical order, with a married woman's maiden name in brackets. The dates following the names are the dates of the issue of The Eganville Leader in which they appeared. The location listed for each person is the place where they spent most of their life, not necessarily where they died.

Budarick, Martin. July 26, 1935. Raglan Township.
Bimm, Ernst F. November 15, 1935. Eganville.
Chusroskie, Simon. October 17, 1930. Wilberforce Township. (Rankin)
Cutchaw, Peter. September 15, 1922. Wilberforce Township. (Lake Dore)
Handke, Charles Oscar. March 29, 1929. Sebastopol Township.
Hoelkie, Charles. July 3, 1936. Augsburg.
Junop, Mrs. Christian. (Hannah Luloff). May 19, 1933. Rosenthal.
Kosmack, Albert. October 31, 1924. Vanbrugh.
Kuehl, William Frderick. March 6, 1936. Woermke.
Liedtke, Bernard. June 24, 1927. Raglan Township.
Lisk, John. August 9, 1918. Grattan Township.
Luloff, John Frederick. April 28, 1939. Golden Lake.
Pahl, Mrs. Julius. (Mathilda Lindemann) June 19, 1936. Wolfe.
Popke, Julius. Nov. 30, 1928. Golden Lake.
Weckworth, Frank. November 9, 1928. Grattan Township.

The Late Mr. Bimm.

The death of Mr. Ernst F. Bimm on Tuesday, November 5th, at his home in Eganville, marked the close of a long and useful life and the termination of an interesting and impressive career. He was one of Eganville's oldest citizens, enjoying the esteem of all in the community,—a man of substance and integrity and one who contributed in good measure to the material advancement of the town as well as being a generous supporter of his church. Mr. Bimm in the exercise of brain and brawn acquired a substantial competency. His successful career could well be cited as an example and as an incentive to a younger generation, and from it the lesson deserved that worthwhile success can only be achieved by labor and application and a commendable degree of thrift. Mr. Bimm "paid his way" and never sought to eke out an existence by evading the stern demands and duties of life and leaving to his fellowmen the burden of his livelihood.

The subject of this obituary was born in Germany in the year 1849. He came to Canada and to Eganville in 1881 and the following year started business as a general blacksmith. His skill as such and his satisfactory dealing with customers were reflected in the growing patronage. In 1911 he established the general store business which is now in control of Bimm Bros. (his sons).

Mr. Bimm's marriage took place in Germany. His wife (Augusta Klingbeil), died ten years ago. Five sons and six daughters are living, namely, Herman, Albert, Ernest, Robert and Kunebert of Eganville, Mrs. E. O. Welk and Mrs. William Kutschke of Pembroke, Mrs. R. G. Reinke, Mrs G. Kersten, Mrs. A Brose and Mrs. R Kasdorff of Eganville. He also leaves forty-two grandchildren and sixteen great-grandchildren.

The funeral was held on Thursday afternoon to Grace Lutheran church and cemetery. All classes and creeds in the community were represented in the large cortege following the remains, and from neighboring centres came groups of citizens to join in the tribute of respect and honor. The services at the church were conducted by the pastor, Rev. M. Voss, who in his English and German discourses paid fitting and deserving tribute to the worth of Mr. Bimm as a head of a family, as a citizen and church adherent. A solemn musical service was rendered. Interment was made in Grace cemetery, the pall-bearers being five sons, Herman, Ernest, Albert, Robert and Kunnibert Bimm, and a grandson, Arthur H. Bimm.

The Late Martin Budarick.

This community mourns the loss of its oldest pioneer in the person of Martin Budarick. He was born in Germany on October 23, 1837; he died July 9, 1935. In 1867 he was married to Annie Risto. Twelve children were born into this home. There preceded him to the grave his loving wife, two sons and one daughter, Christie and Thomas and Caroline (Mrs. G. H. Pilgrim). Living members of the family are: Martin of Cobalt; William, John, Alex. and Daniel of Palmer Rapids, Ont.; three daughters, Elizabeth (Mrs. Peter Wasmund), Mary (Mrs. Henry Mantiefel), Rose (Mrs. G. B. Mantiefel) of Palmer Rapids; one sister, Mrs. Ronald Sealeldt, sr.; sixty-three grandchildren, sixty-seven great-grandchildren and two great-great-grandchildren.

Mr. Budarick and his wife landed in the township of Wilberforce where they made a home for themselves. Later on they sold their property and moved to Raglan, nearly 65 years ago. This upper country at that time was all forest. It meant almost more than human courage to hew out a home, but Mr. Budarick was one of those strong characters. He had a cheerful disposition and always looked on the bright side of life. He cleared one of the nicest farms in this community, which meant a good many hard days. He was always found doing something. He will be greatly missed in his home and by all who were acquainted with him. In his early years he gave his heart to Christ. During the ministry of Rev. E. H. Beau he assumed the offices of Sunday School Superintendent and class leader in the Evangelical Church. He has now gone to the Great Beyond where his life shall be extended forever more. The funeral took place July 11th. Rev. J. M. Oestricher conducted the service and preached, using for his text— St. John 11:25. Sub "Life After Death."

Simon Chusroskie.

After a short illness the death occurred to a respected resident of Wilberforce in the person of Simon Chusroskie, who passed away on Wednesday morning, the 8th inst., in his seventy-fifth year. He was born in Germany and was a son of the late Mr. Anthony and Mrs. Chusroskie.

He came to Canada with his parents when only two years old. About forty-seven years ago he took for his wife Louisa Schmidt and to them ten children were born, five of whom died in infancy. Those who live to mourn his loss besides his wife are three daughters and two sons, namely, Sister M. Clotilde of St. Josephs' Convent, Pembroke, and Sister M. St. Lucy St. Joseph's Convent, Douglas; Simon of Wilberforce and Anna and Lawrence at home. Also, three sisters, Mrs. Christy Kruger of Chapleau, Ont.; Mrs. Edward Huebner and Mrs. Andrew Kutchaw of Pembroke, and one brother, Mr. Anthony Chusroskie, of Cartier.

The funeral, which was largely attended, was held on Friday morning to St. Columba's Cathedral, Pembroke, where the solemn requiem high Mass was chanted by Rev. T. Holy, with Rev. J. A. French as deacon, Rev. J. L. Ennis as sub-deacon, and Rev. Dr. Clarke, master of ceremonies. His body was laid to rest in the family plot in the R. C. cemetery, Pembroke.

The pall-bearers were Michael James Breen, John Charles O'Neill, Michael Connolly, Michael Howard, Francis Kiley and Daniel Tracey.

Centenarian Dies at Eganville.

Peter Cutchaw Attained the Great Age of 103.

The death occurred here on Monday of Peter Cutchaw, who was probably the oldest man in Eastern Ontario, he having reached the remarkable age of 103. He was born in a province of Poland, where he was twice married. Coming to Canada he settled on a farm at Lake Dore with his wife who predeceased him but two and one-half years ago.

He was the father of twenty children, eight of whom are living, namely, Stephen Cutchaw, of Sudbury; Michael, of Pembroke; Joseph, of Rankin; Simon, of Bulger's Corners; Mrs. Julius Nighbor, of Detroit; Mrs. Michael Burke, of Sudbury; Mrs. W. S. Crebasse, of L'Anse, Mich., and Mrs. John Maski, of Eganville. He leaves one hundred grandchildren and fifty great-grandchildren. The deceased spent the past eleven years of his life with his sons and daughters. For three years he was cared for by Mrs. Maski, of Eganville, at whose home he passed away on Monday.

The funeral was held on Wednesday morning at eight o'clock to St. James' church. Requiem High Mass was celebrated by Rev. Father Drohan, who also preached an appropriate sermon. After the Libera was chanted the body was conveyed to the cemetery and laid in the grave. The pall-bearers were Henry Radke, Lorne Wickware, Simon Chusroskie, Sr., John Maski, John O'Brien and Wm. Daley.

Out-of-town friends and relatives attended the obsequies were Mr. and Mrs. Michael Cutchaw, Mrs. Andrew Cutchaw and Mr. Frank Nighbor, of Pembroke; Mr. and Mrs. Simon Cutchaw, Kathleen and Peter Cutchaw and Mr. and Mrs. Simon Chusroskie, of Bulger's Corners; Mr. and Mrs. Henry Radke and Messrs. Joseph Cutchaw and Lorne Wickware, of Rankin.

Many spiritual offerings were placed on the casket.

The Late Charles Oscar Handke.

The death occurred on Sunday, March 17th, at 11 o'clock, p.m., of a well-known and highly respected resident of the township of Sebastopol in the person of Mr. Charles Oscar Handke. Born in Neidorf, County Kruterchine, in the Province of Posen, Germany, on January 6th, 1846, he had reached the ripe old age of 83 years, 2 months and 11 days. In the year 1876 he and his wife, Rose Merzel, and eight children crossed the Atlantic and came to Canada and to Sebastopol in Renfrew County, in which township they have resided ever since. There is a family of two sons and two daughters, namely, Ernest Handke of Eganville, Herman Handke at home, Mrs. Wm. Popp of South Algona and Mrs. Wm. Granzie of Foymount. Miss Dora Klatt of Ottawa is an adopted daughter. Stepchildren are Mrs. Albert Boike of South Algona and August Handke at home. There are twenty-seven grandchildren and twenty-five great-grandchildren.

About thirty-five years ago, the late Mr. Handke worked on the survey of the Grand Trunk railway, then known as the Booth line when the supplies had to be drawn in on handsleighs. He was a great lover of bees and developed quite a honey industry, at times having as many as two hundred hives under his care.

The funeral was held from the home of his son, Herman, to the Lutheran church, of which deceased was a life-long member and thence to the Lutheran cemetery. Rev. Mr. Kasdorf officiated and preached a very impressive sermon. The pall-bearers were Ernest Handke, Wm. Granzie, Wm. Keuhl, Sr., Otto Schrader, Thomas and Michael Kelly.

Charles Hoelkie.

Death has summoned an old and respected resident of South Algona in the person of Charles Hoelkie. He was born in Prussia, Germany, on August 10th, 1854, and had therefore attained the venerable age of 81 years, 10 months and 10 days. He is the last of a family which worthily filled a place in the communities which numbered them among their members.

The late Mr. Hoelkie was married in Germany on the 10th December, 1876, taking for his life partner August Wilhelmina Wolf, who survives.

The couple sailed for Canada on the 4th April, 1881, and after a voyage of six weeks landed at Montreal. Arriving at Eganville Mr. Hoelkie procured employment for two years on the Bonfield farm. He later located on a farm in South Algona and about twenty-one years ago he took possession of a farm home near Augsburg where his death occurred on June 20.

Mr. Hoelkie was a man of a generous disposition and many kindly deeds could be traced to his hands. He was a friend to those in need. In the home he was ever the kind husband and loving father.

Besides his wife he is survived by two sons, Herman Hoelkie of South Algona and Henry Hoelkie at home. His only daughter predeceased him on the 5th April this year. There are ten grandchildren.

The funeral took place from his late home on the following Monday at two o'clock, p.m., to St. John's Lutheran church and cemetery at Augsburg. The large attendance of friends and neighbors showed the high esteem in which deceased was held. The sermon was delivered by the Rev. W. Vetter, who spoke on death and paid a tribute to the departed one. The body was borne to the cemetary by Ernest Risto, August Ott, Ferdinand Hein, Charles Ott, Ernest Shultz and Charles Hein.

ROSENTHAL

Death of Mrs. Christina Junop.

A widely-known and esteemed resident, Mrs Christian Junop (nee Hannah Louise Luloff), died on May 10, 1933, after a brief illness.

Mrs. Junop was a native of the province of Pommern in Gerrmany—born there on November 12, 1854. She came to Canada in 1873, and two years later was married to Mr. Christian Junop. The couple established their home in the township of Raglan. To them were born fourteen children—ten sons and four daughters

She was a member of the Evangelical church at Rosenthal. In her the family have lost a loving mother, the neighborhood a sympathetic friend and the church a strong pillar.

Chief mourners and survivors are her aged mother in Germany, 96 years old ; a loving husband, 6 sisters, 2 brothers, 8 sons and 3 daughters.

The funeral on Saturday, May 13th, was largely attended. A memorial service in the Rosenthal Evangelical church was conducted by Rev. L. H. Pietch, a former pastor, in the absence of the pastor, Rev. J. M. Oestreicher. Interment was made in the Rosenthal cemetery.

Vanbrugh.

The Late Albert Kosmack.

On the 16th October, a well-known and highly respected resident of this community passed away in the person of Albert Kosmack. He had been ailing since early spring and death came as a welcome relief from his suffering.

The body was conveyed to St. John's Evangelical Lutheran church, of Sebastopol, where the Rev. Mr. Kasdorf conducted the funeral service. From there the cortege proceeded to the Lutheran cemetery at Eganville where interment was made. A numerous body of friends and neighbors followed the remains to their last resting place—paying this last tribute of respect and esteem to one whose kindness and courteous manner impressed all who knew him.

The late Mr. Kosmack was born in the year 1842 in the Province of Brandenburg, Germany, and came to Canada in 1860. He was among the pioneers—first settling in the township of Lyndock. There, out of the virgin forest, he cut and hewed a home for himself, and there, also, in 1865, he married Miss Wilhelmina Quade who predeceased him four years ago. Eleven children were born to them, of which eight survive.

In 1874 he moved with his family to Sebastopol and settled on the present homestead now known as Vanbrugh Post Office. The position of postmaster he held for forty-eight years and in this capacity served the neighborhood efficiently and faithfully.

He leaves to mourn his death three sons, Albert of Eganville, Ferdinand of Grattan, and Fred on the homestead, and five daughters, Mrs. Morlok of Eganville, Mrs. E. Wahrlick of Vanbrugh, Mrs. Wolfe of Grattan, Mrs. Bluhm of Wainwright, Sask., and Mrs. Martz of Ottawa ; also, thirty-two grandchildren and five great-grandchildren. May his soul rest in peace.

WOERMKE.

William Frederick Kuehl.

After a life of service to his family and to the community in which he lived, a worthy and respected resident of Sebastopol paid the debt of nature, and laid down the combined burden of old age and prolonged illness and entered into his rest and reward on Sunday, February 16th.

Deceased was born in Rowenstein, Germany, on August 31st, 1864. In 1883 he with his parents crossed the Atlantic to America and took up residence in Grattan. A year later a farm home was purchased in Lyndock township where they took up their permanent abode He worked hard to earn a livelihood for himself and family.

In the year 1893 he led to the marriage altar Miss Johanna Heideman, who proved a true helpmeet in matters spiritual and material throughout the forty-three years of their married life.

The worthy couple were blessed with eleven children, seven of whom are living, namely, William, John and Louis, of Sebastopol ; Anna (Mrs. William Schweigert) of Clontarf ; Amelia (Mrs. Otto Zoschke) of Eganville ; Mary (Mrs. Joseph Musclow) of Clontarf ; Elizabeth (Mrs. Albert Rosien) on the homestead. Selma (Mrs. August Reinert) preceded her father to the grave seven years ago. Three children died in infancy. Besides his widow, three sons and four daughters, he leaves to mourn twenty-seven grandchildren and one great-grandchild.

The last twenty years of his life were spent in Sebastopol—a faultless citizen, a faithful Christian and church member, a true friend to all, a loving husband and father—the late Mr. Kuehl is greatly missed and mourned.

The funeral was held on Wednesday morning from his late home to the St. John's Lutheran church and cemetery, Sebastopol, and in spite of the bitter cold was attended by many friends from far and neighbors of the family. The services were conducted by Rev. W. Vetter. The pall-bearers were his two sons, William and John, and four sons-in-law, William Schweigert, Otto Zoschke, Joseph Musclow and Albert Rosien. All the family were present at the obsequies.

Death of Bernard Liedtke of Raglan.

On Monday, June 13th, 1927, at Montreal, there passed away one of Raglan's most worthy and estimable residents in the person of Mr. Bernard Liedtke, whose removal has created a sense of profound and widespread grief.

For several years he had been a victim of an internal malady, and, on several occasions had sought treatment from different physicians. Finally, he decided to consult a specialist, and about two months ago accompanied by his wife and sister-in-law, Mrs. W. Rahm, of Arnprior, he journeyed to Montreal and entered the Royal Victoria Hospital. There all that medical skill could devise was done to prolong his life, but all efforts proved futile.

Deceased was born on November 12, 1868, in the village of Jamee, Province West Prussia. On December 5, 1883, he left his homeland, came to Canada in company with his parents and settled in the township of Raglan, where he since resided. In 1901 he chose for his partner in life Miss Helena Rahm, daughter of J. Rahm of Denbigh. The union was blessed by eleven children, five of whom are dead.

The subject of this obituary was a man of most attractive personality, was widely known, served in both township and county councils, and numbered many close personal friends. Among the people with whom he lived he was honored and revered by all for his generosity and many neighbourly acts. He was a prominent figure in many ways—making a success of the numerous things to which he applied himself. He bore an excellent reputation in the community which knew him from childhood until life's sands ran out. His name was synonymous with trustworthiness, probity, charitableness and fidelity to principle. A true husband and devoted father, the separation caused by death brings in its train keen sorrow and a sense of irreparable loss.

Besides his sorrowing wife he is mourned by four sons, two daughters and three sisters, The funeral, which was held on Friday afternoon, was the largest ever seen in this district, testifying to the high esteem in which deceased was held.

Among those from a distance to attend the funeral were Mrs. A. W. Rahm of Arnprior, Mrs. C. Funk of Montreal, Mr. and Mrs. Chas. Genrick, Mr. and Mrs. J. Zadow and Mr. Wm. Genrick of Pembroke, Mr. and Mrs. A. Millark, Mr. and Mrs. R. Millark of Golden Lake.

The pall-bearers were Michael Moore, P. J. Windle, O. Schutt, C. Marquardt,

The Late John Lisk.

After a lingering illness, borne with Christian patience and resignation, Mr. John Lisk, Sr., passed away on Friday evening last here at the home of his son, Mr. John Lisk, Jr. The deceased was born in Drauchausen, Germany, in May, 1841. When a young man he crossed the Atlantic to the United States, and subsequently, in the early 60's, settled in Grattan township where he lived and labored and brought up his family. About twelve years ago he retired and with his wife came to Eganville, to the home of his son. The late Mr. Lisk was known as an industrious and trustworthy man, fulfilling his obligations as husband, father and citizen in an exemplary manner. Those who have known him best, the life he lived, the work he did, will be the first to acknowledge that he had the desire to serve his generation.

Besides his venerable helpmeet he has a family of seven sons and four daughters, namely, Messrs Fred Lisk, of Killaloe; William, of Golden Lake; Henry, of Australia; Herman, of Grattan; John, Albert E. and James Lisk, of Eganville; Mrs. James Leonard, of California; Mrs. D. Halley, of Bancroft; Mrs. W. A. L. Smith, of Eganville and Nursing Sister Minnie Lisk, overseas.

Deceased was a faithful member of Melville Presbyterian church, and thence the funeral was held on Sunday afternoon at three o'clock, there being a large attendance of relatives, friends and citizens in general. Burial services were conducted by Rev. Mr. Hendrick, of Golden Lake and Rev. G. W. Mylne, pastor of the church. The pall-bearers were six sons of deceased.

Death Removes Well Known Resident of Golden Lake.

The death of John Frederick Luloff, of Golden Lake, which occurred on Thursday last at the home of his sister, Mrs. John Luloff, of Mud Lake, removes from earthly scenes a member of a family which was among the first to settle in the Golden Lake section. He was a son of John Frederick Luloff and his wife, Ernestine Kregor, born in Germany on May 14, 1869. As a boy of eight years he came to Canada with his parents, the family settling on a farm at Golden Lake. As a youth he attended the government school on the Indian Reserve and later a Public School when one was established in the locality. As he grew to manhood the late Mr. Luloff took a keen interest in church administration and municipal affairs. He became superintendent of the Sunday School and was a leader of the church choir. He was an unwavering supporter of the Liberal party and could discuss with knowledge and intelligence the greater problems of national life. Mr. Luloff was a frequent caller at this office and from these contacts it was discernible how his quiet humor and quaint philosophy were factors in gaining for him many enduring friendships.

The late Mr. Luloff was a farm worker, maker of wagons and coffins and was not unskilled as a builder. He was unmarried. Surviving brothers and sisters are Mr. Herman Luloff and Mr. Edward Luloff of Golden Lake and Mrs. John Luloff of Grattan. There are five living nephews and nieces. A brother predeceased him in 1934. He had been living with his sister since last November and had been in his usual health until the first week in April when he suffered a stroke. On Thursday night, the 20th inst., the final summons came.

The funeral was held on Sunday afternoon to the Evangelical church and cemetery at Golden Lake. There was a large assembly of friends from over a wide district, come to pay a tribute of respect to one who had played a worthy part in the building up of the community in which he lived. The services were conducted by the Rev. Gross, and the choir renderings added to the impressiveness of the occasion. Burial was in the Evangelical cemetery, the pall-bearers being Amiel Neitzel, Herman Junop, Albert Mundt, Leonard Heiderman, August Noach and John E. Luloff.

Death Calls One of Eganville's Oldest Residents.

William Michaelis, Sr., for close on fifty years a resident of Eganville and a worthy and most respected citizen, lay down the burden of four score and three years on Friday afternoon last. The end came rather suddenly. Though confined to a sick room, he had been able an hour before his death to converse with Rev. L. Smith, pastor of Melville United church, and members of his family. Then, without any indications of pain or suffering, he entered his long sleep.

The late Mr. Michaelis was born in the Province of Brandenburg, Germany, on July 5, 1842, the son of Frederick Michaelis and his wife Sophia Bimm. The period of the Franco-Prussian war in 1870 found him tailoring for the soldiers in a German garrison. Receiving his discharge at the close of the war, he crossed the Atlantic to join in Canada his parents and family who had preceded him ten years. From Sand Point to Eganville he travelled by stage coach. On the homestead in south Algona he continued his work as a tailor for five or six years. In 1876 he married Amelia Kaddatz, of Sebastopol, and in the following year the young couple came to Eganville to reside. Their first place of abode was the Colin Campbell hotel (now the Dover premises) where they remained for a year, and then he purchased the Peter O'Farrell property where he remained until the end. His wife predeceased him thirty-four years and of a family of five children (one son and four daughters) three are living: Mr. T. William Michaelis, of Eganville; Mrs. Wm. J. Wolfe, of Windsor, and Mrs. A. Lavelle, of Pembroke.

Down through a long stretch of years Mr. Michaelis applied himself without interruption to his work as a tailor. His life was quiet and uneventful, and though his lot was cast among a people to whom he was alien in race and creed he would confess he lived with them in peace, harmony and good will. Mr. Michaelis was a Christian gentleman of a high order of intelligence, a worthy citizen who maintained always most agreeable relations with his neighbors, and who as a husband and father discharged his duties in the most commendable manner. He was a faithful adherent of the Presbyterian church and for a period of eleven years, up to the time of his death, was an elder of Melville church here.

The funeral was held on Sunday afternoon at 2.30 o'clock, outside services being conducted at the house by Rev. Mr. Smith, who also paid an eloquent and deserving tribute to the fine qualities of mind and heart of deceased. All classes and creeds in the community were largely represented at the funeral, evidencing thereby the high esteem in which the deceased was held. Interment was made in the family plot in Melville church cemetery. The pall-bearers were the Board of Management and Elders of the church, Messrs John Lisk, Jas. Moore, Geo. Reeves, Wm. A. MacGregor, John Sutherland and Ira Whelan.

An Old Resident Called by Death.

Julius Popke, one of the oldest residents of these parts, passed away on Tuesday morning here at the home of his son, Mr. William Popke. For years the old gentleman had his home close by the Golden Lake road. There he cultivated his garden and there as a blacksmith and gunsmith he achieved a widespread reputation as a very skilled workman. He was a familiar figure to the people of Eganville and Golden Lake and all entertained the most kindly feelings for the old gentleman who was spending his last years in philosophic contentment and peace.

Deceased, who would have reached his 93rd year this coming December, was born in Germany, and there he married Dora Prange. After eleven years of married life, the couple left their native land and came to Canada. For a time they resided in Eganville and then established a home near Golden Lake. Mrs. Popkie died thirty-six years ago. Four sons and one daughter are living: William of Eganville, Walter of Cobalt, Ernest of Kirkland Lake and Robert in Saskatchewan, and a daughter living in Timmins. One brother, Mr. Edward Popke, of Grattan, survives.

The late Mr. Popkie bore arms for the Fatherland, being a soldier in service in the war of 1870-71 between Germany and France. He is the last of the soldier comrades who settled hereabouts.

The funeral was held yesterday afternoon to Grace Lutheran Church and to Germanicus cemetery.

The Late Mr. and Mrs. Julius Pahl.

Pioneer Settlers in Township of Brudenell.

(Communicated)

With the death of Mrs. Pahl which occurred on Friday, June 5th, there passed to the Great Beyond one of the pioneer and respected residents of the Wolfe section of the township of Brudenell. Her short illness she bore with great patience. While yet a girl she gave her heart and life to the Master, whom she served faithfully until her death.

Mrs. Mathilda Pahl, nee Lindemann, was born on the 22nd of October, 1856, at Bussow Kr. Friedburg, Prussia. In 1872 she came to Canada with her parents who settled in Arnprior. In that town she was married to Julius Pahl who preceded her to the grave two and a half years ago. The young couple settled in the township of Brudenell in 1882 and under the pioneer conditions which then prevailed applied themselves earnestly and perseveringly to the task of establishing a home. With an industry that did not cease or tire they succeeded. Seventeen children were born into the family, eight of whom are living, seven sons and one daughter, namely, Otto and John Pahl of Balgonie, Sask.; Charles, Julius, Frederick and Joseph of Findlater, Sask.; Herman Pahl on the homestead in Brudenell township, and Mrs. Joseph Boicey, of Renfrew. There are 53 grandchildren, 13 great-grandchildren and one great-great-grandchild. Numerous friends and acquaintances regret to learn of her death. Mrs. Pahl was an ideal mother for her family and the example of her life will be long enshrined in their hearts. She was always the good, helpful neighbor to others in their hour of sickness or need, and her advice was often sought.

The funeral service was held under the direction of her pastor, Rev. David Lettke, from the home of Mr. Herman Pahl to the Lyndoak Baptist church and cemetery.

The family wishes to thank all friends for their kind sympathy during their recent bereavement.

The Late Frank Weckworth.

On Tuesday, 23rd October, at the home of his son, Otto, a well-known resident of Grattan passed away in the person of Mr. Frank Weckworth. He was born in the Province of Pommern, Germany, on August 30, 1858. When he attained the age of twenty-four he married Augusta Knop who died in 1900. Mr. Weckworth was married a second time, to Anna Neumeyer who passed away on Christmas eve, 19.7.

The deceased came to Canada with his family in November, 1903, and settled in the township of Grattan. Of ten children born of the first marriage, six are living, namely, Paul of Syracuse, N.Y ; Mrs. H. Saar of Stafford, Ernest of Pembroke, Otto of Grattan, Mrs. Wm Mittlesteadt, Eganville, and Frank of McAdam; N B. Twelve children were born of the second union and eleven are living : Mrs. H. Kohlsmith of Strathroy, Eric on the homestead, Mrs. Wm. Connaghan of Grattan, Mrs. D. Faulkner of Britannia Bay, Mrs. H. Schuneman of Rankin, Mrs O. Sperberg of Lake Dore, Freda, William, Elizabeth, Kurt and Vera at the home of Otto Weckworth. His living grandchildren number thirty-five.

The funeral was held on Friday, October 26th, to Grace Lutheran church, Eganville. Rev. M. Voes, pastor, conducted the services. Interment was made in Grace cemetery, the pall-bearers being his sons, Paul, Ernest, Otto, Frank, Eric and William. All the members of the family were present with the exception of Mrs. Kohlsmith.

Floral offerings were received as follow: Pillow from Mr. Frank Weckworth and family, Cross from Mr. Otto Weckworth and family, Cross from Mr. and Mrs. H. Saar, Wreath from Mr. Paul Weckworth and family, Spray from Mr. and Mrs. Wm. Mittelsteadt, Wreath from Freda, William, Elizabeth, Kurt and Vera (children), Spray from Mr. and Mrs. Wm. Connaghan, Wreath from Mr. and Mrs D. Faulkner, Spray from Mr. and Mrs. Eric Weckworth.

Index

The following list of surnames, compiled from the text and the cutlines, contains some that are not German in origin. Obviously, the immigrants who spoke a different language did not live in Renfrew County in complete isolation. Their lives were touched by government officials, businessmen, ministers, school inspectors, census-takers and also farmers who were British or Anglo-Canadian in background. Most of the names, though, belong to the immigrant families who were German-speaking, and whose presence in this part of Canada has been recorded in this book.

Alles, Rev. Peter, 12, 105
Allum, Rev. Carl (Charles) 11, 12
Antler, Charles, 98
Antler, Emile, 98
Antler, Rudolph, 98
Arno, Jon W., 64
Ashick, Mrs. Raymond, 70
Bahm, 17
Balsteadt, A., 98
Barker, John, 98
Bartscher, George, 40
Batz, W., 47
Becker, Fredericka, 28
Behnke, August, 98
Behnke, Fred, 98
Berger, William, 91
Bergur, 13
Berndt, W., 28
Bernt, W., 47
Biderman, A., 47
Biederman, J., 47
Biedermann, William, 55
Biesenthal, 10
Biesenthal, Adolph, 86
Biesenthal, Caroline, 65, 83
Biesenthal, Clara, 86
Biesenthal, Della, 86
Biesenthal, Ferdinand, 12, 65, 66, 70, 83, 86
Biesenthal, Martha, 86
Biesenthal, Rev. Walter, 96
Biggs, Cassie, 86
Bimm, Ernst, 13, 40, 110, 111
Bismark, Otto von, 21
Blaedow, Fred, 98
Blaedow, John, 45
Blaedow, William, 98
Blank, Doreen, 88
Blank, Leonard, 88
Blech, John, 98
Blemkie (family), 74
Blimkie, Mary, 35
Blimkie, Martin, 35
Blimkie, Michael, 35
Blimkie, Paul, 35
Blodow, J., 47
Bochert, Charles, 37, 49
Boehme, August, 13, 64, 71, 77
Bohn, J., 47
Bohn, John, 52
Born, Anistina, 57
Born, Christian, 57, 59
Born, Louisa, 57
Born, William, 57, 59
Borutski, Phyllis, 88
Borutski, Ronnie, 88
Borutskie, Antoine, 45

Boshard, Jacob, 12
Boubrie, 13
Bowes, Charles, 25
Bramberger, Gotlip, 55
Brandenburg, 17
Brasch, Albert Carl, 48
Brasch, Wilhelm Ferdinand, 55
Bredlau, H., 47
Brindle, James, 98
Brose, 17, 59
Brose, Donna, 88
Brose, E., 47
Brose, Ernst, 59
Brose, P., 47
Brown, 13
Brown, Dr. Caroline, 100
Brumm, Charles, 98
Bucholtz, Alex, 86
Bucholtz, Dora, 86
Bucholtz, Gertie, 86
Bucholtz, Minnie, 86
Buckwald, Mr. and Mrs. Ferdinand, 13, 15
Buckwald, Gustave, 15
Buckwald, Henrietta, 15
Buckwald, Otto, 15
Budarick (Boudrick, Budarich) Martin, 12, 13, 32, 52, 54, 110, 11
Budd, Wesley, 14, 29, 58, 68
Budd, Mrs. Wesley, 49
Budd, Mr. and Mrs. Wilhelm, 10, 58
Budd (family), 68
Budder, John, 55
Budher, Martin, 55
Burgess, Thomas F., 101
Burgomeister, Friedrich B., 27
Burke, August, 55
Burwash, Nathaniel, 41
Butt, Carl, 98
Butt, J., 47
Byers, Wilherlmina, 17
Christink, Irving, 82
Chusroskie, 25
Chusroskie, Simon, 110, 111
Cobourn, Miss Minnie, 86
Condie, James, 41
Cutchaw, Peter, 110, 111
Demand, William, 98
Demant, Johann Carl, 104
Denzion (family), 13
Digulla (family) 92, 93, 96
Doering, Paulina, 55
Drefke (family) 39
Drefke, Verner, 40, 43
Druve, William (Wilhelm) 67

Egan, John, 41
Eggert, Bruno, 32
Eisenstein, C., 8
Ewit, 13
Felske, G., 47
Ferguson, W., 49
Fick, Gustave, 25, 67
Fick, Wesley, 26
Fick, Mr. and Mrs. William Frederick, 25, 50, 67
Fiss, 17
Fitzner, Wilhelm, 12
Forgie, J., 98
Frantz, 13, 17
Frederick, Charles, 12
French, T.P., 21, 23, 32, 33, 41, 52
Fridrick, W., 47
Frietag, Bertha, 66
Frivalt, Florence, 86
Gahr, R., 47
Geiser, 17
Genrick, Arthur Karl Bernhard, 32
George, W., 55
Gerber, Herbert, 109
Gerndt, Rev. Ludwig Herman, 11, 12, 16, 102
Gierman, Adeline, 18
Gierman, Gottlip (Gotlieb) 13, 24
Gieser, 17
Golberg, Martin, 98
Goldt, Carl, 26
Goldt, Ferdinand, 26
Gorr, Charles, 98
Gorr, Henry, 98
Gorr, Johann Wilhelm (William) 22, 30
Graham, Ray, 86
Graham, Stanley, 86
Gransey, 13
Grief, C., 47, 51
Grief, Otto, 98
Griefe, H., 47
Gries, John, 12
Griese, 13
Grife, Mr. and Mrs. Adolph, 62, 70, 80
Grife, Emma, 70
Groehl, Daniel, 32
Groehl, John, 32
Grohl, D., 47
Groshles, 13
Guenther, Miss Isabel V., 86
Gust, Albert, 98
Gust, August, 36, 72
Gust, Fred, 98
Gutzeit, Friedrich August, 64, 66, 70
Gutzman (Goodsman) Alfred, 11
Gutzman, August, 34
Gutzman, Carolin, 34
Gutzman, Charles (Carl), 34, 43, 52, 70, 78
Gutzman, William, 34, 78, 79
Haas, Julius, 75
Hahs, H., 47
Haiss, 13
Hain, A., 47
Hain, J., 47
Hampel, Gustav, 98
Handke, Charles Oscar, 110, 111
Hartwick, Mrs. Jean, 90

Hass, Henry, 86
Hass, Sam, 86
Hayes, M.P., 21
Heideman, Christian, 16
Hein, Robert August, 33
Hienz, 17
Hildebrandt, C., 47
Hildebrandt, Karl, 51
Hildebrandt, William, 16
Hine, A., 47
Hine, W., 47
Hinz, 17
Hoch, Gustave, 109
Hoelke (Hoelkie) Charles, 57, 110, 111, 112
Holly, John, 45
Holterman, F., 33
Horcun, Anna, 8
Horcun, Lise, 8
Horcun, Maria, 8
Horcun, Matthew, 8, 19, 45, 56, 57
Hunt, H., 47
Jeffrey, Teresa, 88
Jenson, P., 100
Junop, Mrs. Christian, 110, 112
Junop, G., 47
Jurgans, Mrs. Jacob, 98
Kaija, Anthony, 88
Kaija, Lorraine, 88
Kant (family), 92
Kant, David, 94, 96
Ferdinand, E.O., 17, 94, 96
Kant, Otto, 93
Kapakaski, 13
Kappele, Rev. Stephen, 12
Karow, W., 47
Kelo (family), 70
Kelo, John, 67
Kelo, Solomon, 57, 76
Kessatz, Fred, 98
Keuhl, Glen, 88
Kirsch (Kirk) August, 69
Kirsch, Augusta, 69
Kinder, Ellis, 108
Kizell, Jacob, 50
Klingbeil, Erna Augusta Frederika, 110
Klingbeil, Myles, 88
Klingbeil, William, 61
Kohl, F., 47
Kolmaier, D., 47
Komm, F., 47
Kopke, C., 47
Kosmack, 39
Kosmack, Albert, 16, 18, 40, 110, 112
Kosmack, Allan, 18, 41
Kosmack, Morley, 41
Kosmack, Frederick, 18, 40
Krantz, G., 47
Krohn, Johann, 69, 73
Krone, H., 47
Kruger, Adolph, 91, 95
Kruger, Albert, 91
Kruger, August, 25, 52, 91, 92, 93, 94, 96
Kruger, Mrs. August, 52, 92
Kruger, Bill, 91
Kruger, Ernest, 91
Kruger, Frank, 52, 91, 95
Kruger, Mrs. Frank (Annie) 94
Kruger, Joseph, 91
Kruger, Martin, 28

116

Kruger, Mary, 91, 93
Kruger, Paul, 91, 96
Kuehl, William Frederick, 110, 112
Kulke, Caroline, 12
Kurth, Fred, 98
Kurtguey, 13
Kutchke (Kutzcke) H., 47
Laman, A., 47
Lang, August, 12, 54, 55
Lang, Charlotte, 55
Lang, Glenda, 88
Larose, Ronnie, 88
Lau, Alma, 34
Lau, Alvina, 34
Lau, Arthur, 34
Lau, John, 34
Lau, Verner, 34
Lau, Zelma, 34
Lebeck, Martin, 55
Lebow, 17
Leman, J., 47
Lemke, Mr. and Mrs. William, 53
Lenser, Martin, 59
Lenser, Otto, 59
Lett, Ralph, 54, 55
Liebeck, Sam, 68
Liedtke, Audrey, 88
Liedtke, Bernard, 110, 112
Liedtke, David, 88
Limerand, 13
Lindeman, Ferdinand, 12
Lipke, A., 47
Lipke, August, 32, 104, 107
Lipke, Eric, 107
Lipke, Frank, 107
Lipke, Johann, Gotlieb, 25, 74, 104, 107
Lipke, Wilhelmine, 25
Lisk, John, 110, 113
Lisk, William, 45
Lubo, H., 47
Lubow (family), 106
Luloff, A., 47
Luloff (Anna Wilhelmina Louisa (Mrs John)) 37, 38
Luloff, Bill (Wilhelm) 22, 67, 79, 109, 110
Luloff, E., 47
Luloff, Edward, 22, 38
Luloff, Ernestine (Mrs Johann) 22
Luloff, Ferdinand, 22, 38
Luloff, H., 47
Luloff, Herman, 22
Luloff, Johann, 22, 38, 64, 69
Luloff, John, 28, 37, 38, 53, 110, 113
Luloff, Sarah, 67
Luloff, Teresa, 79
Luloff, Wilhelm, 32
Madigan, 29
Markus, Martin, 56, 57, 58
Mashke, 17
Mau (family) 10
Mau, Dora, 86
Mau, Herman, 86
Maves, William, 51, 66
McCauley, George, 86
McDonald, Peter, 25
McDonald, Steven, 88
McDougall, John Lorne, 41
McNab, Inspector G.G., 89, 90
McRae, J.D., 40
Merrick, Charles, 41

Michaelis, Auguste Ernestine, 78
Michaelis, Mr. and Mrs. William J., 11, 110, 113
Michel, Bruno, 15
Michel, Caroline, 8, 15
Michel, Emil, 15
Michel, Gustave (Gustav) 8, 11, 14, 15, 34, 56
Michel, Oscar, 14, 26, 34
Michel, Robert, 15, 26
Michel, Mrs Robert, 56
Mickael, 17
Millark, Donnie, 88
Miller, A., 47
Miller, Mrs. James, 88
Miller, Mr. and Mrs. Wilfred, 92
Mills, R.P., 60
Milroy, Michael, 34
Moffatt, Alexander, 41
Mohns, August, 98
Mohns, Fred, 98
Moller, Gottlieb, 52
Montgomery, Alex, 98
Montgomery, Struthers, 86
Moritz, W., 47
Morlock, Fred, 16
Morlock, George, 16
Morris, Mayor J.L., 99
Mueller, August, 68
Mueller, Theresa, 63
Murray, T.W., 98
Musclow, 13, 16, 17
Nauman, J., 47
Neuman, August, 12
Niewman, 13
Noack, Albert, 45
Noack, August, 45
Noack, Johann, 75
Noack, Matthew, 45, 105, cover
Noack, William, 45
Okum, Matthew, 45
Ott, Adolph, 55
Ott, Mrs Adolph (Hertha) 53
Ott, Gusta, 62
Otter, Major-General Sir William, 96, 97
Pahl, Mrs. Julius (Mathilda) 110, 114
Phanenhaur, Charles (Carl), 14
Pfannenhour, 13
Phitzner, 12
Pilatske, Edgar, 107
Plaunt, Xavier, 47
Popke, Julius, 110, 113
Popp, 17
Potter, Carl (Charles) 32, 108
Potter, Dorothee, 108
Prange, Gus, 98
Psaow, P., 47
Quade, August, 14
Quade, Wilhelmina, 18
Quast family, 96
Quast, Alma, 23
Quast, B., 47
Quast, Christian, 23, 52
Quast, Frederick, 23, 95
Quast, Mrs. Frederick, 23
Quast, Gotlieb, 23, 52
Quast, John, 23, 95
Quast, Wilbert, 23
Raddatz, Henry, 34
Radtke, Emma, 86

Radtke, Sam, 86
Radtke, T., 47
Radtke, William, 100
Radtkie, Charles, 98
Radtkie, John, 98
Raeder, Roy, 88
Raglin, C., 47
Reaman, G. Elmore, 24
Reckzin, G., 47
Reckzine, W., 47
Redtman, Robert, 44
Reeves, George, 89
Reiche, Caroline, 33
Reiche, Erdman, 33
Reiche, Frederick, 33
Reiche, Walter, 32, 33
Reicher, E., 47
Reinke, R.G., 76
Remus, Julius, 28
Richter (family) 92, 93
Richter, Mrs. Jean, 17
Rickzen, E., 47
Rieglen, H., 47
Ringel, Carl, 32
Ristau, Arnold Sr., 35
Ristau, Mrs. Arnold, 53
Ristau, Arnold Bernhard (Barney), 31, 32, 107
Risto, Ernest, 86
Risto, Frank, 86
Rose, Rheinhold, 16
Rosien (Rosin) Karl, 16, 34
Roy, William, 34
Ruhs, Carl, 32
Runtz (family) 75
Runtz, Charles, 107
Rusler, E., 47
Ruslir, J., 47
Saar, Earl, 106
Saar, Johann Frederick Ernst, 106
Sack, Frank, 47
Sarsfield, James, 98
Schauer (family) 61
Schauer, Carol, 88
Schauer, Grant, 88
Schauer, Julius J., 89
Schauer, Kenny, 88
Schimmen, H., 47
Schiscoske, F., 47
Schleuter, Keith, 8, 45
Schmidt, Rev. Karl, 11
Schmidt, William, 16
Schonfelt, H., 47
Schonfelt, W., 47
Schroder, August, 52
Schroder, J., 47
Schroeder, Rev. C., 85
Schroeder (family) 58
Schroeder, August, 98
Schroeder, Mrs. Ormal, 89
Schroeder, Mr. and Mrs. William (Petawawa Twp.) 36
Schroeder, Mr. and Mrs. William (S. Algona Twp.) 23, 52
Schroider, 13
Schruder, Frank J., 101
Schultz, Albert, 26
Schultz, Emilia, 35
Schultz, Ernest, 29
Schultz, F., 47
Schultz, Herman, 29
Schultz, J., 47
Schultz, R., 47
Schultze, August H.J., 13

Schultze, Mrs. Karl, 72, 80
Schunaman, E., 47
Schutt (family) 13
Schutt, Bernhard, 47
Schutt, C., 47
Schutt, Christian F., 14
Schutt, Frederick (Friedriche) 32
Schutt, Gerhard, 47
Schwanz, Paul, 26
Schwartz, Carl, 22
Schwartz, Caroline Wilhelmina, 22
Schwartz, Wilhelmina, 22
Schweig Martin, 54
Schwegert, Richard, 16
Scott, Inspector R. George, 85, 86
Seafield, 13
Sell, Elizabeth, 62
Sell, Friedrich, 52
Sell, Fritz, 62
Sell, Jo., 47
Selkirk, William, 98
Seller, August, 16
Shurman, Mr., 52
Siegle, C., 47
Sill, F., 47
Sill, H., 47
Sill, O., 47
Sinn, William, 7, 19, 30, 41, 49, 52, 60
Smith, John, 25
Sperberg, A., 47
Spreeman, Fred, 98
Springer, W., 47
Stashnick, J., 47
Stein, Charles, 41
Stein, Paul, 41
Sterndorf, Christian Albertina, 67
Sterling, Karen, 88
Sterling, Lennox, 88
Stresman (family) 68
Stresman, Annie, 86
Stresman, Gustave, 29
Tackman, Charles, 33
Teske, Johanna, 24
Teske, John, 24
Tennant, George, 98
Thom, 13
Thur, Frederick, 29
Thur, Leanne, 88
Tiegs, Mrs. Eleanor, 39
Tierney, J., 49
Tierney, W., 49
Timm, Bertha, 59
Towns, 13
Tur, F., 47
Vankoughnet, Hon. Peter, 21
Verch, Edmund, 68
Verch, Mrs., 63
Verch, Louis F., 68, 71
Verch, William, 63
Vertlieb, Moses, 94
Vollrath, Charles August, 65, 106
Wagner, William, 7, 17
Walters, 13
Walther, William, 44
Wasmund, Christian, 13, 17, 32
Watson, John, 32, 41
Weckworth, Frank, 110
Wegner, August, 98
Wegner, Henry, 98

117

Weisenberg, William, 98
Weissenberg, 36
Whelan, John, 34
White, C., 91
White, Inspector E.T., 88
White, Richard, 38
Wienhols, W., 47
Wieland, Brenda, 88
Wienke, Charlotte, 99
Wienke, Elsie, 87, 99, 100
Wienke, Wilhelm, 99
Wiessenberg, Frederick, 64, 65
Wills, W.J., 18
Wilson, Andrew, 13
Witt, Friedrich, Preface, 10
Witzel, H., 47
Wodtke, John, 14
Woermke, Mrs. Gottlieb, 14, 18
Woito, Fred, 98
Woito, Martin, 98
Wolfgram, Caroline, 12
Wolfgram, Eliza, 54
Wolgram, Frank, 47
Wolfgram, Friedrich, 54
Wolgram, H., 47
Wolfgram, Herman, 45
Wolfgram, W., 47
Wolfgram, William Frederick, 12, 25, 86
Wolkenstein, 17
Woller, S., 47
Wright, H.W., 60
Yake, Julius, 75
Yandt, Fred, 70
Yant, Herman, 12
Yante, F., 47
Yeas, Henry, 32
Yeas, Mrs. Henry (Rose) 48, 55
Zadow, August, 27, 78
Zadow, Driscoll, 27
Zadow, Eddie, 78
Zadow, Edward, 101
Zadow, Mrs. Edward, 15, 27, 78
Zadow, Gertrude, 78
Zadow, Louise Auguste, 78
Zadow, Julius Albert, 9, 43, 64, 78, 101
Zadow, Mrs. Walter, 53
Zadow, William, 52, 78
Zebel, Christopher, 12
Zeise, 17
Ziebarth, Edward, 16
Ziebarth, Julius Eduard, 32
Zillmer, Charlotte Auguste Kreuger Zadow, 7, 27
Zimmerman, Rev. Louis D., 86
Zohr, Roy, 88
Zosche, Ferdinand, 16.